FOREW...
DANIEL P...

CW00543498

19

Humbled

THE KEY TO God's VISITATION

CARLOS ANNACONDIA

CfaN CHRIST
FOR ALL NATIONS

Australia • Brazil • Canada • Germany • Hong Kong • Singapore
South Africa • United Kingdom • United States • West Africa

Humbled
The Key to God's Visitation

© 2019 by Carlos Annacondia – *Mensaje de Salvación*
www.CarlosAnnacondia.com

Published by:
Christ for all Nations
P.O. Box 590588
Orlando, FL 32859-0588
www.cfan.org

ISBN: 978-1-933446-82-0 (Paperback)
ISBN: 978-1-933446-83-7 (E-book)
ISBN: 978-9-875576-73-5 (Spanish)

Interior Design: *Grupo Nivel Uno, Inc.*
Cover Design: *DesignsToGo.net*
Project Manager: *Sam Rodriguez*
Editorial Proofing: *Rick Kern*

Printed in the United States of America

Acknowledgements

I would like to express my heartfelt thanks to my wife, Maria. She has been, and continues to be, the ideal helper and I'm so grateful that Jesus has placed her by my side. Over these many years while I have been away serving the Lord conducting evangelism campaigns, she has supported me with her prayers. Several times a year these campaigns would be extremely lengthy taking me far from home between forty and seventy days without a break.

From our headquarters (our home), she built an altar of prayer and devotion to God, never failing to trust in Him. And with nine children, she had quite the task guiding them in their studies, correcting them, and training them—all while keeping our home spotless. She has faithfully been there to meet me at airports, service stations, or at our doorway, always with a loving smile. She has never complained about the amount of time that I have had to spend away from her and our children.

Although she has often had to stay behind with the family, her heart has always been with all the wonderful things that the Lord has done through our evangelistic events. She would often pack our kids into the car and drive thousands of miles so the family could spend a weekend together during a distant campaign.

The only reason I am able to share all the amazing things that God has done as I speak at conferences, seminars, or write in magazines and books, is because Jesus has placed my beloved wife as an angel to support me. Thank you Maria! You make up more than half of the ministry that Jesus gave us in 1981.

I also want to Thank Moses and Sabrina, my son and daughter-in-law. They have worked tirelessly and unwaveringly to collate the messages that I have given over the years.

To our beloved Savior, Lord of all, be glory and honor forever!

ABOUT THE AUTHOR

Carlos Alberto Annacondia was born in the city of Quilmes, Argentina close to its capital, Buenos Aires. He and his beloved wife, Maria, have raised a family of nine children, and to date, enjoy thirteen grandchildren.

On May 19, 1979, Carlos gave his life to Jesus and from that time on, a passion for preaching the Gospel has captivated his heart.

Shortly after surrendering his life to Christ, in 1981, he began his ministry as an evangelist, preaching the message of Jesus in the slums of Greater Buenos Aires. He has travelled to many countries, boldly sharing the life-changing message that transformed his life and family.

THE REASON FOR THIS BOOK

The story opens ove three decades ago immediately after I had received the baptism of the Holy Spirit. Suddenly, I supernaturally began to see people's overwhelming need and it filled me with a tremendous sense of sorrow and compassion. In response, the Holy Spirit led me into sustained periods of intense prayer where I would spend lengthy stretches of time alone in the presence of God. Weeping and crying out for the needy people that God had shown me, the experience took hold of me and changed my life forever. King David expressed a similar sentiment when he declared "I am worn out from my groaning. All night long I flood my bed with weeping and drench my couch with tears." (Psalm 6:6)

I can remember those times of prayer as though they occurred yesterday. Being a new Christian, I didn't understand why those things were happening. I would spend hours kneeling by my bed, weeping and crying out to God to the point that the sheets were soaked by the time I finished.

That season of praying, weeping, and crying out for the needs of the people went on for quite a long time. As I knelt humbled and surrendered in God's presence, He showed me there was something important that I could do for all the needy people I was praying for. Then I understood the purpose of being humbled and unconditionally surrendered to His call.

The deep humbling that I experienced enabled God to reveal His plan for my and my family's lives to me. It was something that I could never have imagined or invented. From that place of humility, the Lord began to reveal a clear purpose that would change the course of this simple businessman's life forever.

The Bible declares: "If my people, who are called by my name, will humble themselves and pray and seek my face and turn from their wicked ways, then I will hear from heaven, and I will forgive their sin and will heal their land." (2 Chronicles 7:14) What a wonderful truth for the times we live in when we need an open heaven so desperately.

Beloved Church of Jesus Christ, the only way to be fruitful in God is to be humbled and walk in complete, unconditional surrender before the King of kings. We have to realize we are nothing without Him—that deep within we need and long for Him. Our heart's desire as believers is to follow in His footsteps, presenting Jesus to a world that is groaning in agony of spirit without Him.

However, before the world can be touched by God, the Church has to first be touched in a deeper way itself. And for this to happen, we need to learn to be humbled in God's presence.

–Carlos Annacondia

TABLE OF CONTENTS

INTRODUCTION

In God's book, the Bible, the Apostle Paul proclaims, "For I am not ashamed of the gospel, because it is the power of God..." (Romans 1:16a) God gives this Gospel of power to all who dare to trust in Him and His Word, and who believe that everything written in His Word is Yes and Amen, forever and ever.

Accordingly, this book presents to every man and woman a challenge to believe in the power of God for salvation, deliverance, healing, restoration, and victory here on earth. God is a God of love and power. He demonstrated this through His Son Jesus Christ, who shed His precious blood for us all on the cross of Calvary, rejecting no one. His love and power reach all who dare to trust and believe in Him.

God wants you to experience each of the testimonies that you read in this book. He has done these things in our lives over the years since my husband and I gave our hearts, our lives, and everything that we have to Jesus. Over the last thirty-years, the Lord has never failed us or our family. He remains faithful in every situation that we go through no matter how difficult it is. We have experienced His love and power in our marriage as God has taught us to forgive each other, understand each other, and to love each other.

Together with our children, we have been guided and taught to trust Him as we have matured in the fear and love of the Lord. And when sickness or problems have come against us, the Lord has shown us each day that the only way to receive His blessings is by trusting in His power and His promises. These are for all His children—those who choose to live according to His Word.

May this book be a source of inspiration and blessing for each one of you.

–Maria Annacondia

FOREWORD

As a teenager I volunteered to work on the prayer team for one of Carlos Annacondia's evangelistic crusades in Orlando, Florida. I had heard stories about his ministry for years and I had read his well-known book, *Listen to Me Satan*, but nothing could have prepared me for what I witnessed.

After the altar call had been given, Evangelist Annacondia began to take authority over demonic spirits, commanding them to leave in Jesus name. "Fuera, fuera!" ("out, out") He shouted. "Ahora, ahora" ("now, now") "En el nombre de Jesus" ("in the name of Jesus"). I was slightly surprised that demons also knew Spanish. Then again, even someone who didn't know Spanish, like myself, could recognize the authority in his voice. All over the building demons manifested. We carried those demonized into an adjacent room and prayed with them until they were totally free and born again!

Years later friends of mine who had visited one of Carlos Annacondia's crusades in Argentina told me that when they first arrived someone asked them if they wanted to know the key to this move of God. They were led behind the platform, and when they looked underneath the stage they could see intercessors—including Carlos himself and his wife Maria—interceding fervently for souls.

As I have come to know Evangelist Annacondia and his family, I have been so impressed by their humility and passion for God and people. They have not lost the fundamentals that made their ministry so powerful. They are still in the midst of a mighty move of the Spirit, even after so many years. What an amazing example they are to us.

In Matthew 13:52, Jesus said, *"Therefore every scribe who has been trained for the kingdom of heaven is like a master of a house, who brings out of his treasure what is new and what is old."* Jesus contrasted the scribes, whom he often rebuked along with Pharisees and Sadducees, with scribes in the Kingdom of Heaven. The former group simply copied old writings. But Kingdom scribes are different. They are not simply human copy machines. They are masters of a house in which there is a treasure room full of truth at their command. They are able to bring forth priceless treasures to give and to impart at will.

As we follow Jesus in discipleship, those lessons we learn in the Spirit become treasures we own.

Those things we have discovered as we have paid a price to walk with the Holy Spirit over mountaintops and in down in deep valleys—they are more than bible studies—they are treasures. No one can take them from us—we own them. But we can give them to those with hungry hearts.

Paul told the Romans that his ministry in their midst had the ability to impart gifts that would make them strong (Rom. 1:11). Paul also told the Philippians, who were connected with him in ministry and sat under his teaching, that they were partakers in his grace (Phil. 1:7). It is an amazing thought that we are actually able to tap into the grace, the supernatural empowerment, upon someone else's life—simply receiving from them.

When I read a book like this one, from a man like Carlos Annacondia, I don't see it as merely a Bible study. I see it as a treasure from a disciple of Jesus who has paid a price to follow Him over many years and many decades. What he learned at so great a price, he offers through this book for anyone who will simply open their heart, humble themselves and receive.

Someone said, "You teach what you know, but you reproduce what you are." When it comes to the treasures in this book, you can rest assured that you are receiving from a man who lives what he teaches and who has seen great fruit as a result of these principles. If you put them to practice in your life, you will see great fruit also. As you read this book, read it with an open heart. As you do, you will receive a gift and become a partaker of supernatural grace. May the Holy Spirit use the truth on these pages to impart a gift to you that will establish and strengthen you.

–Evangelist Daniel Kolenda
Christ for all Nations

PREFACE

I opened my eyes to the glare of the world for the first time on March 12, 1944. The second of Vicente Annacondia and Zunilda Alonso's three sons, I lived the first years of my childhood and adolescence in a very normal home. When I was only ten-years old, I learned the meaning of the words work and determination, though it was of necessity, not choice.

Once I had matured and found a stable job, I met my future wife, Maria, and we soon decided to get married. Over the years our family grew and we were able to enjoy our own home. Though we were financially comfortable compared to other average families, it was only when I was thirty-five-years old that I really started to live. I may have been born thirty-five years earlier, but on the 19th of May, 1979, I was born again. This was the day of my spiritual birth—the day I asked Jesus to come into my life. And merely a week after accepting Jesus as my Savior, I was baptized in the Holy Spirit.

From that moment on I was filled with a consuming passion to tell the whole world about the Jesus who had transformed my life, my family, and all that I am! This gave new purpose and meaning to my life. Today, thirty-two years later, that same passion continues to fill everything: my life, my dreams, my plans... This amazing call from God has taken me around the world to tell the nations, peoples, and languages, about Jesus—the One who died and rose again for us to give us the victory for eternity.

The Bible teaches us how beautiful and breathtaking this task of evangelism is, emphasizing its vital importance for our Lord Jesus Christ. When I read what has become known as "the Great Commission" in the Bible, I am reminded of the supreme task we have to evangelize. As the body of Christ, it falls to us to rise up and "go!" Go into all the world—to announce, proclaim, and tell everyone that He is the way, the truth, and the life.

The Gospel of Mark puts it this way, "He said to them, 'Go into all the world and preach the gospel to all creation. Whoever believes and is baptized will be saved, but whoever does not believe will be condemned. And these signs will accompany those who believe: in my name they will drive out demons; they will speak in new tongues; they will pick up snakes with their hands; and when they drink deadly poison, it will not hurt them at all; they will place their hands on people who are ill, and they will get well.'" (Mark 16: 15-18)

During my many years of ministry since 1981, I have noticed with sadness how the Church throughout the world has often disregarded this command. For some, the task of evangelism has become a burden while for others it has become a duty—just another event in the journal. Thinking of evangelism in this way is sure to lead to failure which is why I decided to write this book! In the light of God's Word, I want to share what He has taught me about the meaning of evangelism over the years.

As the Church of Jesus, we must understand that the great task of evangelism is a call to engage in spiritual warfare. Simply stated, evangelism is putting spiritual warfare into practice. It is going out from the four walls of our church into the enemy's territory, the battleground we call "the world," into the squares, parks, and streets... It is the call to go to the places where Satan is in control, where he rules and where he keeps people in slavery to sin. It means going out from the comfort and safety of our headquarters, where soldiers are prepared for battle, to conquer and occupy the enemy's territory. More than that, evangelism is taking hold of the souls that the devil has held captive and tear them right out of his claws.

The verses from Mark 16:15-18 mentioned earlier give us a clear mission. And when that mission is joined with the strategy revealed in 2 Corinthians 4:3-4, it can be carried out using the tools mentioned in Ephesians 6:10-18. Furthermore, we, the Church of Jesus, have the authority to command the devil to release the souls he holds bound so that the Gospel can shine throughout all the earth. The Word of God not only gives us the call, it shows us the problem and offers the solution. That being said, however, it is up to us to actually *do* what the Bible says.

I pray that a passion for evangelism will take hold of your life. May you understand, be conscious of, and able to exercise the authority that God has given you to defeat the devil, so that many can come to know Jesus. May you become a Christian who prays passionately for those who have a deep need to know the Savior. Today more than ever we need to cry out to God for the needy, and at the same time go out and seek them.

"Lord Jesus, may the words of this book inspire many to take Your Word and go out in the authority You have given us to see the results that You have promised us… Amen!"

CHAPTER 1

The Secret to Revival

PART ONE

One day I found myself talking to American Evangelist Stephen Hill and his wife, Jeri. During the course of our conversation, they shared something that they had experienced during a visit to one of our evangelism campaigns in Argentina. Among the reasons this couple had come to Argentina as missionaries, was to visit one of our evangelism campaigns. They had heard about the remarkable move of God that was unfolding in Argentina, and wanted to see the incredible conversions that had been reported for themselves. For those of you who may be unaware, Stephen and Jeri Hill were missionaries in southern Argentina for several years. After they returned to the United States, the Holy Spirit used them in the revival He brought to Pensacola that touched the whole world.

One evening while they were in Argentina, Stephen and Jeri visited one of our evangelism campaigns. They hadn't told anyone about their reason for being there, but as they wandered through the crowd, they were approached by someone who asked them rather directly, "Would you like to know the key to the spiritual victory that you can see here?" Their immediate response was, "Of course!"

Their benefactor then guided them through the crowd to the back of the large raised platform from where the Gospel was being preached. Peering under the platform they could see hundreds of people, including my wife, Maria, who were spending many hours in intense intercession; praying, weeping, moaning, and crying out to God. As they looked on, their companion, whom they were never to see again, said to Stephen and Jeri, "Here you have the key, the secret to what is happening here."

From the beginning of our ministry God showed us that intense prayer and intercession were a vital part of the spiritual victory that He would give us. When I heard this story, the Lord reminded me again of this precious truth. Much has been said about prayer and we know that there are different ways of praying and different forms of prayer. I would like to share about a type of prayer called intercession with you.

Intercession is born at the very altar of God when a believer kneels with a heart that is suffering for lost and hurting souls through seeing a world that is heading for destruction and without hope. When we look into the Word of God, we find teaching about what true intercession is.

The Fire that Burns Continuously

Leviticus 6:12-13 tells us, "The fire on the altar must be kept burning; it must not go out. Every morning the priest is to add firewood and arrange the burnt offering on the fire and burn the fat of the fellowship offerings on it. The fire must be kept burning on the altar continuously; it must not go out."

The duty of the priest was to keep the flame lit. "Every morning" he had to place firewood on the altar. There is still an altar that is aflame, a personal altar that is ignited through intercessory prayer. It is set ablaze as we pray for our own needs, for our family, for our country, for our government, for the Church, and for those who are suffering...

What I'm getting at is that this same principle is valid for our lives today even though our ministry is different from the priests of the Old Testament. Each morning we must rekindle the fire on the altar. If we let the fire go out, we fail to obey a precept that God explains in His Word. It is essential that we maintain our personal altar, keeping our devotion to God alight—we cannot let it go out for any reason.

Many times the rush and countless demands of everyday life cause our prayer life to become a duty. We only have time to pray "Lord, bless this day. Watch over my life and my family. Amen." But God is looking for something more. Keeping the fire burning involves more work than just coming to the altar.

It is known that fire is one of the main elements in the fight against the impurities, germs, and micro-organisms that are harmful to our health. Additionally, it is said that "Fire kills everything" and the same applies to the fire on the altar—it burns everything. When we place ourselves in front of the altar, before its blazing flames, the Lord deals with all our impurities.

God is looking for men and women who are prepared to get on their knees before Him, concerned not only with their own needs, but interceding for those who are suffering. When we do this, our prayer reaches the very throne of God.

As we turn our lives toward the Lord, we must seek to enter His presence, reaching His inner throne room. That is the place where all the army of heaven worships Him day and night. It is there that angels, archangels, cherubim, seraphim, and elders fall before the Lord, and together with them, we throw ourselves at the feet of Jesus. When we realize in our hearts that we have reached that special place, it is difficult to hold back the tears knowing with certainty that He is listening to us.

GOD IS LOOKING FOR PRIESTS

The Lord has raised us up to be kings and priests. We seem to have a good understanding of our roles as kings, with all the privileges and benefits that we can enjoy as well as the promises we rely on. But Revelation 1:6 reveals that there is also a priesthood. This passage declares "and has made us to be a kingdom and priests to serve his God and Father..."

We find it easy to accept that we are reigning with the Lord Jesus, who has placed us in a position of authority where we can enjoy the riches and blessings of His Kingdom. But what the Lord is searching for in this crucial hour is priests. He seeks those who are willing not only to enjoy His blessings, but to sacrifice themselves for others. He longs for those who will plead for the souls of the lost alone in the secret place, not in the presence of others to gain their spiritual esteem or applause. The intercession of these saints lays hold of eternity in the battleground of their prayer closet where no one sees what they are doing. Nor does anyone notice when they lose their voices feverishly crying out as they demand that the devil releases the souls which he holds in bondage.

Our duties, functions, privileges, and responsibilities as Christians are like a two-edge sword: On the one hand we are kings, (as many of us endeavor to be), but on the other hand we are priests. And what is the function of the priest? Simply stated, a priest is someone who puts himself between God and man, taking responsibility for the sins of the people. Ezekiel 22:30 put it this way, "I looked for someone among them who would build up the wall and stand before me in the gap on behalf of the land so I would not have to destroy it, but I found no one."

God is looking for brave men and women who are prepared to lay down their lives before Him, and who are not content to just enjoy His blessings. In the Scripture we have many examples of true priests. We find Moses who, on repeated occasions as we read in the following passages, presented himself before God to cry out for his people:

"Moses returned to the Lord and said, 'Why, Lord, why have you brought trouble on this people? Is this why you sent me? Ever since I went to Pharaoh to speak in your name, he has brought trouble on this people, and you have not rescued your people at all.'" (Exodus 5:22-23)

"Then Moses cried out to the Lord, 'What am I to do with these people? They are almost ready to stone me.'" (Exodus 17:4)

"So Moses went back to the Lord and said, 'Oh, what a great sin these people have committed! They have made themselves gods of gold. But now, please forgive their sin—but if not, then blot me out of the book you have written.'" (Exodus 32:31-32)

"The people came to Moses and said, 'We sinned when we spoke against the Lord and against you. Pray that the Lord will take the snakes away from us.' So Moses prayed for the people." (Numbers 21:7)

When the people were hungry, Moses cried out to God. When the people were thirsty, Moses interceded for them before the Lord. Whenever the Israelites found themselves in trouble and suffering, there was Moses burdened by all the needs of the people, taking responsibility for them before God.

Daniel was another faithful priest for God. Although he himself had not committed the sins of the people, he owned them as if they were his, and cried out to God for forgiveness as he fasted, wept, and covered himself in ashes.

"So I turned to the Lord God and pleaded with him in prayer and petition, in fasting, and in sackcloth and ashes. I prayed to the Lord my God and confessed: 'Lord, the great and awesome God, who keeps his covenant of love with those who love him and keep his commandments, we have sinned and done wrong. We have been wicked and have rebelled; we have turned away from your commands and laws.'" (Daniel 9:3-5)

"Lord, in keeping with all your righteous acts, turn away your anger and your wrath from Jerusalem, your city, your holy hill. Our sins and the iniquities of our ancestors have made Jerusalem and your people an object of scorn to all those around us. Now, our God, hear the prayers and petitions of your servant. For your sake, Lord, look with favor on your desolate sanctuary." (Daniel 9:16-17)

And we could talk about many others such as Abraham, Deborah, Jeremiah, Joel, Elijah, and other people who placed themselves in the breach before the Lord, to cry out for others.

The Prayer that Pleases God

Using a parable, Jesus taught us that although there are many ways to pray, there is one prayer that touches the heart of God in a very special way. The Scripture gives a good example of it in the Gospel of Luke, "Two men went up to the temple to pray, one a Pharisee and the other a tax collector. The Pharisee stood by himself and prayed: 'God, I thank you that I am not like other people—robbers, evildoers, adulterers—or even like this tax collector. I fast twice a week and give a tenth of all I get.' But the tax collector stood at a distance. He would not even look up to heaven, but beat his breast and said, 'God, have mercy on me, a sinner.' I tell you that this man, rather than the other, went home justified before God. For all those who exalt themselves will be humbled, and those who humble themselves will be exalted." (Luke 18:10-14)

Prayer is more than coming before God to bring requests in a carefree and indifferent manner. It's pouring out our hearts before God with tears, knowing that we are nothing before Him. Just like that publican who could only weep and beat his chest, as he cried out for forgiveness. An intense prayer from the heart is the one that receives an answer from God. Many times our prayer is just a series of words, something that comes from the mind and is diluted with a measure of superficiality. But we can only practice deep intercession when we have seen and felt the sufferings of those for whom we are interceding.

How I can pray for a drug addict if I have never seen one dying in a hospital, or never felt for a mother desperately seeking help for her addicted son? We know that when drugs get into a home, they destroy not only the addict which they enslave with their chains of darkness, they also tear the family apart through the pain and suffering inflicted upon those who love the addicted one.

I cannot truly intercede for someone who is imprisoned by alcohol unless I know or have seen the savagery that exists in a home where someone is an alcoholic. The whole family suffers violence, anger, and unspeakable pain from seeing the destruction of their loved one.

When I pray for marriages or for families, the first thing that comes to my mind is what I have seen hundreds of times in campaigns—children crying, tugging at my sleeve in desperation, pleading with me to pray that their mom or dad would come home so that they can have a family again. Then I know how to ask, how to pray, how to intercede. It is not difficult for me to groan, because I am envisioning and identifying with the consequences of a broken marriage. I feel the same when I go to a hospital and approach a stretcher to pray for a suffering patient.

We will not be able to intercede unless we connect with that cry of pain in a way that allows us to feel their anguish and sense the deep tormenting sobs of someone who is suffering. Then the cry of their heart will form on our own lips. Unless we can see the misery in their faces as they await death, and hurt with those people who are suffering, crying from the pain of their illness as they ask us for help—we cannot effectively intercede for them.

If you are willing to intercede, get yourself a large handkerchief because you're going to drench it with tears. When we feel the pain and suffering of others, the least we can do is cry out to God with tears and groans. But as we do, we must bear in mind that the Word of God promises, "Those who sow with tears will reap with songs of joy." (Psalm 126:5)

Some think the secret is in the time spent in prayer. But the number of hours spent repeating words is not what counts. The issue is quality, not quantity—what counts is the way that we pray, where our hearts are at. I place more value on one or two hours spent crying and groaning in intense prayer than on eight or ten hours spent praying prayers with which no-one agrees.

THE WORLD IS GROANING WHOM SHALL I SEND?

It was in times of intercession that God gave me a vision. I saw before me a jelly-like globe that was beating like a heart. From the inside of this "little world" were coming howls, screams of terror, panic, pain, despair, cries of someone who was being raped or was dying; dreadful sobbing and screaming of all kinds. In the middle of all this I heard a voice that said, "The world is groaning. Whom shall I send?" Three times over I heard the same voice cry out. After I'd heard the voice three times, I remember saying, "Lord, send me. I'll go." Of course, I could not imagine what would happen later on. All I said was, "Lord, send me."

God still has the same expectation as He looks for people who are willing to sacrifice their time, not only to preach the Gospel, but also to intercede, to groan, to cry out, and to weep for those who are in need. The Bible teaches that Jesus himself prayed before the Father in this way, "During the days of Jesus' life on earth, he offered up prayers and petitions with fervent cries and tears to the one who could save him from death, and he was heard because of his reverent submission." (Hebrews 5:7)

Let's take our Savior as our supreme example and begin to pray, cry out, groan, and weep with loud cries and tears for those who are lost. Let's not let a day pass without this being a reality in our lives.

CHAPTER 2

The Secret to Revival

PART TWO

Over the years as the Lord has guided us, we have come to realize that the spiritual warfare so many speak about is not some formula or process that can be taught through academics. Neither is the enemy engaged through a series of steps that we have to learn and apply. Many have taught on this topic, and dozens of books have been written about it. However, I have discovered that the majority of people do not actually speak from experience but instead talk about what they have heard or think that they know.

Many are the methods and strategies that are used to wage the spiritual battle, but the truth is that spiritual warfare begins with intercession. It is something that is only born deep down in a person's heart after they have seen and identified with another's pain. Then that person can enter into a struggle, not against other people, but against Satan and his army.

Why do we refer to this as "spiritual warfare?" When we speak of warfare in human terms we mean some form of combat; a fistfight, a hand-to-hand clash, a firefight, a battle to take a city or advance on a beachhead—some sort of violent physical confrontation. The conflict is similar in the spiritual realm as we engage the devil and his minions in combat.

The only difference between fierce conflicts that take place in the spiritual realm and the hostilities occurring between nations for example, is largely abstract. Physical combat between armed forces and warring factions use all kinds of weaponry from sticks-and-stones to highly advanced technology. Human battles rely on armament and munitions such as machine guns, rifles, bombs, and sophisticated missiles or weapons systems, etc... In fact, soldiers will employ any instrument that can harm the opponent as needed. Conversely, our conflict does not need physical weapons because as 2 Corinthians 10:4 explains, "The weapons we fight with are not the weapons of the world. On the contrary, they have divine power to demolish strongholds." Our battle begins with prayer and intense intercession.

Prayer: The Key to Spiritual Warfare

I could tell you many stories about the various spiritual battles that we have had, about the fierce attacks of the devil and God's faithfulness. For every onslaught ended with the Lord finally giving us the victory when we stopped to intercede and fight against the devil's army.

We know perfectly well that our struggle is not against people or human institutions. Many times as Christians we get confused and involved in all kinds of arguments. That being said, who is the one that throws the wrench into the works and holds the Church back? It is Satan! Behind people, laws, or governments that try to stop the preaching of the Gospel is the devil—Satan. Ephesians 6:12 tells us "For we do not wrestle against flesh and blood, but against principalities, against powers, against the rulers of the darkness of this age, against spiritual hosts of wickedness in the heavenly places." (NKJV)

A biblical example of what I am saying is found in the Book of Daniel, "Then he continued, 'Do not be afraid, Daniel. Since the first day that you set your mind to gain understanding and to humble yourself before your God, your words were heard, and

I have come in response to them. But the prince of the Persian kingdom resisted me twenty-one days. Then Michael, one of the chief princes, came to help me, because I was detained there with the king of Persia. Now I have come to explain to you what will happen to your people in the future, for the vision concerns a time yet to come.'" (Daniel 10:12-14)

Note what the angel said to Daniel: "But the prince of the Persian kingdom resisted me twenty-one days." Now a human prince could not resist an angel. So then, what sort of prince is he talking about? He's referring to Satan. The spiritual prince who was ruling over Persia and who had authority there was resisting what God had commanded in response to Daniel's need. The same thing happens today; in every city there is a hierarchy of principalities and powers that resist the will of God for His children.

If you really want to see victory in your life, you will have to fight against these spirits of unbelief, against these demons which try to stop the blessing of God from reaching His children. But consider how this works, "Since the first day that you set your mind to gain understanding and to humble yourself before your God, your words were heard." (Daniel 10: 12)

"Set your mind to gain understanding" speaks to feeling the pain and the need of the person for whom we are praying firsthand. "Humble yourself" means to pour out your heart before God as you identify with drug addicts being torn apart by the devil, marriages being destroyed, or children abandoned... It means crying, groaning, and interceding with tears and pain for those who are suffering. When this happens, God mobilizes all His army and begins to break the chains and tear down the barriers of the devil. We have the authority to pray in this way so that we can defeat our enemy and take back what Satan has robbed from us.

We need to be keenly aware of the following principle: *We have the legal right to claim and take back what the devil has stolen from us. God granted this right to us through His victory on the cross of Calvary.*

If we fail to gain the victory over these principalities through prayer and intense intercession, then the light of Christ will never shine out. We might have some measure of blessing, but we will never enjoy the depth and breadth of victory or blessing that God desires for us. We can only defeat our enemy, the devil, by humbling ourselves, weeping, pleading, crying out and commanding, "devil, loose the souls that you are holding captive, loose the drug addicts, loose the sinners!" and by engaging in battle in the name of Jesus.

One day, we were in the city of Tucuman, Argentina with all the equipment that we had brought from Buenos Aires. We had tents, seating, platforms, and lighting—everything necessary to conduct a crusade... We also had a lot of unexpected problems with the arrangements!

When we arrived at the former airport that the City Council had promised us as the site for our evangelism campaign, we were shocked and deeply distressed upon being told that it was no longer available. The excuse we were offered was that the area was needed because the municipality was going to build a new park there. Needless to say, the park was never built.

Unexpectedly, we found ourselves in Tucuman with all of our equipment, but without a venue for our campaign. A local Christian offered us the use of a site, but it was quite a ways from the center of the city which is where we wanted to conduct the event. Furthermore, the location was beset by poor communication capabilities and inadequate transportation links. But since it was the only option that we had, we decided to hold our campaign there. I felt very discouraged by what was happening—the struggle had begun...

Because the site of the campaign was out of the way, we thought we could still reach the people of the city by broadcasting the meetings on local television stations. Regrettably, this request was turned down leading us to reach out to radio stations. Similarly, we hoped to do radio broadcasts of the meetings, but this led nowhere, as they were all asking for enormous sums of money, and would not even consider our offers.

It seemed as if all the forces of the enemy were mobilized against us—we couldn't get anything organized. All we had was a field with an uneven surface which needed to be cleared before we could even use it. Additionally, there were no public transportation services to the site so whoever did decide to come to the campaign would have to make their own way there and that was no easy task.

Publicity was a huge issue and we realized that people would not be aware of the campaign unless we could broadcast the meetings by television or radio. When we have a campaign site that is in a prominent place, people who are passing by can see what is happening and respond. That's why we always choose locations close to the center of the city. It permits people to become aware of what is taking place allowing them to attend if they choose. But it wasn't going to be like that in Tucuman because the site we now had was completely out of view.

As we contended for what we believed was God's will, a tremendous spiritual battle ensued. Our custom in every campaign was to pray and bind the strong man, the principality over the area (just as Daniel spoke of). We mobilized our forces and stormed the strongholds of hell! Rebuking the enemy, in the name of Jesus we commanded Satan to loose the souls, the homes, the drug addicts, the marriages, the prostitutes, the criminals, and all sinners who were in his grip.

We prayed in the same way for the media. Our plan was to have a meeting with media representatives and put forward our proposal. But first, we spent several days in prayer, withstanding the enemy, and commanding Satan to loosen his grip on the media. We realized that our battle was not against the media bosses, but against the powers, principalities, rulers of the darkness of this age, and the spiritual hosts of wickedness in the heavenly regions. And for that reason we didn't need to argue with the media bosses.

HUMBLED, CRYING OUT AND ASKING FOR FORGIVENESS

Once the crusade started, we decided to try to reach an agreement with the media bosses again. It was impossible to pay the is they were asking. Our intercession now had a clear objective as we asked the Lord to touch the hearts of those who were in charge of the media. We prayed that He would move them to give us affordable rates so the city of Tucuman could hear the Gospel by means of radio and television. Additionally, we kept demanding that the devil loosen his hold on the media.

We struggled for several days engaging in fierce times of spiritual warfare only to have the media turn down our offer again. They lowered their prices somewhat, but their rates were still excessive. In the midst of this battle, with the evangelism campaign in progress, some sisters from our ministry who were praying and interceding for us in Buenos Aires received a vision from God. In their vision, they saw the city of Tucuman surrounded by flames, which were preventing us from entering. They also noted that the ground inside the circle of flames was coloured red.

Once we heard about this vision, we asked the Lord to reveal its meaning. He showed us that the red which stained the ground represented the blood of multitudes that had been shed in the past. The region of Tucuman was the scene of some of the bloodiest warfare to occur during the guerrilla insurgency of the 1970s. We then understood that we had to break the curse over the region arising from this bloodshed, and seek God's forgiveness for what had taken place.

Deciding to gather together Christians who had served in the armed forces during the guerrilla hostilities, we also brought in others who had been members of the guerrilla opposition. The various parties from the terrible conflict were represented at our prayer meeting. We came together to seek God's forgiveness, so that the Lord could heal the land and enable the Gospel to be proclaimed freely.

The Lord heard us and the result was that the radio and television stations suddenly became available. They offered us rates that we could afford, enabling us to broadcast on the television stations and four radio stations.

It wasn't long before people started coming to the campaign on horseback, in carts, in trucks, in buses, on bicycles, and on foot.

Around forty-thousand people visited the site every day thanks to what they had seen on television and heard on the radio. When we gave the altar call, people literally came running to the front. Some people were seriously ill and so desperate for help that they were brought to the meetings in their bed clothes. The campaign ended up being a tremendous success. Day after day we saw precious souls coming to the feet of Jesus and God was glorified as captives were set free and powerful miracles occurred.

If we had not engaged in spiritual warfare, but just waited quietly or passively for something to occur, I doubt that anything would have happened. Instead, because we prayed, interceded, rebuked and bound both the devil and the strong man of Tucuman, we were able to see thousands and thousands of people make the decision to follow Jesus during a campaign that continued for an amazing forty-five nights.

GAIN UNDERSTANDING AND HUMBLE OURSELVES BEFORE GOD

We need to gain understanding about whatever it is that we are praying for. We cannot pray in a way that is detached from the situation. The prayers that God desires from us are those which are born deep within, and come from knowing the pain of those for whom we are praying. When we sense the pain of someone who is suffering, when we feel it first hand, then our intercession changes and God responds.

A church that doesn't fast or pray, that doesn't weep, is an indifferent church. People will not come to the church unless there is someone there who can beat their chest like the publican in the parable told by Jesus, as they cry out to the Lord "God, have mercy on us, for we are sinners." The spiritual battle must be fought on our knees, groaning and crying out to God with tears and weeping. This is how God will know that we long to gain understanding and to humble ourselves, just like Daniel humbled himself. And as we do, He will send his angels to fight for us that we might win the victory.

The Strong Man Has Already Been Defeated

We also had many struggles in the Argentine city of Santiago del Estero when we conducted an evangelism campaign there. Even before the event began, we had to field major problems. We had been given permission to use a strategic location in the center of the city and that address had been featured in all our advertising material. This had been going on for some time so that everyone in the city would be well aware of what was going to be happening.

The problem arose because our advance work convinced the state church in the city to stage their own event at the same location sometime before our campaign was due to begin. So a charismatic priest, who believed in miracles and prayed for the sick, came to an event on the site prior to us, and many local people attended.

About two weeks before our own campaign was to launch however, another priest led a meeting in the same place but this time it was different. This guy was a parapsychologist who was quite the opposite of the charismatic priest who had spoken about miracles. This priest asserted that it was all nonsense, that miracles did not happen, and that the powers of darkness were the products of human imagination.

So there had been quite a spiritual upheaval prior to our arrival leading to an atmosphere that was not at all conducive to carrying out an evangelism campaign. And the local evangelical church, which was quite small in number, was really distressed and concerned about what had happened. From a practical point of view, it seemed that nothing we were planning would be of any impact. However, we decided to go ahead with the campaign.

We had the same struggle with the media that we had experienced in the city of Tucuman. Satan had them under his control and he didn't want to let them go. While negotiations with the media bosses went on, we kept interceding and demanding that the devil let go of the radio and television. There was no way that they wanted to broadcast the campaign and we were not in a position to pay the price that they were asking. Once again, we began the intercession battle, praying, groaning, weeping, and demanding, "Satan, loose the media in the name of Jesus!" We went on like this for several days, morning, afternoon, and evening. It was a pitched battle, waged by travailing prayer and no other means.

WHAT SPIRITUAL WARFARE IS NOT...

At this point I would like to digress and share an experience to illustrate this point. On one of my trips to Europe, I visited a major city where I met with local believers. As we stood at the front of a church in the city, they told me how they had already implemented many "spiritual strategies," as they called them, but somehow none of them had worked. Groups of them had circled the city by car as they interceded, they had prayer walked their city; they had prayed in front of the major shrines, statues, and monuments, in order to break the covenants that had been made through them. They had even flown over the city, praying from the air but none of their efforts had made a difference. So when I arrived, the first thing they asked me was: "Why did none of this work?"

My response was simple; "I believe that encircling a city in prayer has been done before, in the city of Jericho, where it was commanded by God. According to my understanding, it is not the act of encircling a city that brings victory, but the prayers of believers on their knees who are crying out to God. With broken hearts we must weep and groan commanding Satan to, 'Loose the city, loose those that you are holding captive, the drug addicts, the alcoholics, loose the marriages that you are destroying!'"

Interceding in this way for those who are suffering is what makes the difference. Encircling a city in prayer doesn't change anything because the battle is not against brick and mortar any more than it is against flesh and blood, but against principalities. Satan has to get his filthy hands off, and loose the people that he is holding captive.

I have already explained to you what needed to be done. I don't want to belittle someone else's strategy, but I believe that intercession is the strategy that is found in the Bible. This is what the priests of God were doing when they placed themselves between God and the people in order to cry out for them. Intercession is what Jesus did in the Garden of Gethsemane, as described in Luke 22:44, "And being in anguish, he prayed more earnestly, and his sweat was like drops of blood falling to the ground." During that prayer millions of souls were snatched from the clutches of the devil, perhaps our own souls included. This is the kind of intercession that is extremely effective, and we must put it into practice.

And it is exactly what we did in the city of Santiago del Estero, commanding Satan in the name of Jesus to loose the city, its people, and the local media. We were staying in the middle of a residential neighborhood and began praying early each morning. And although we tried to keep the noise down, it was impossible to hide the fact that we were interceding from the neighbors as we cried out for the city. We couldn't help weeping and travailing in prayer as we ordered the devil to get out of the city.

During one of those days of intercession, a brother in our team received a vision. In it he saw Satan seated on a throne that was shaking and bumping as if an earthquake was taking place. The next day, God gave the same vision for a second time. Two or three days later, we received a different vision during our intercession meeting, and this time I also saw it. I remember seeing a vast army of miniature Roman soldiers, rather like dwarfs, who were running from one side to the other. They were running north, south, east, and west, not knowing where to escape. What struck me most was seeing all their weapons scattered on the ground. There were all kinds of weapons—sticks, shields, spears, swords, and even javelins, all scattered on the ground as the soldiers ran around chaotically.

Then I asked the Lord, "What is all this about?" Immediately the Holy Spirit responded "The strong man is bound." I asked another question, "But why are the little soldiers running about? Lord, why are they disoriented, not knowing what to do?" "Because the princes have been bound, and the soldiers can no longer receive orders," answered the Holy Spirit. This meant that the leaders had lost control of their soldiers, who no longer knew what to do or where to attack. "And why are the weapons lying on the ground? I asked again. "Because they have been defeated, and a defeated army flees and abandons its weapons," came the reply.

This made sense to me because if soldiers flee taking their weapons with them they are planning to return and continue the fight. They have not been defeated, and once they have regrouped they will attack again. But the army we saw in the vision had been defeated.

From that moment on, we were able to do radio and television broadcasts of the evangelism campaign, because the media had been set free. People came to hear the Gospel by the thousands, running to receive Jesus. Even those who just happened to be passing the campaign site in buses or cars were touched by the power of God. They would come running in, weeping as they cried out to the Lord for forgiveness.

A few days later, something really strange happened. A large group of people got together to try and oppose what we were doing. They arranged for the statue of a saint to be carried in a procession around the neighborhood where we were holding the evangelism campaign. As the procession crossed the street in front of the site of our meeting, the four people carrying the statue were knocked to the ground by the power of God and the statue itself was shattered as it fell. The people who had been walking behind the statue in the procession began to scream and experience demonic manifestations. The Lord worked powerfully!

The anointing and power of the Holy Spirit was so formidable that we had to arrange early morning meetings so that everyone could attend. People came from all over the region because they had watched the campaign on TV. The day we started the morning meetings, eight-hundred people committed their lives to Jesus for the first time.

The result was that tens of thousands of people came to the feet of Jesus. Spiritual warfare, prayer, and intercession are what made the difference. I'm convinced the outcome would have been quite different if we had not engaged the enemy in battle and if we had not taken by faith, that which God was giving us. If we had not groaned in prayer, and rebuked the devil, the results would not have been as significant. However, God gave us the victory.

So how do we gain the victory? By waging war in the heavenly places for ours is a spiritual battle. As Ephesians 6: 12 says "For we do not wrestle against flesh and blood, but against principalities, against powers, against the rulers of the darkness of this age, against spiritual hosts of wickedness in the heavenly places." (NKJV)

WHAT THEN IS SPIRITUAL WARFARE?

Spiritual warfare works in a specific way. In physical warfare, air attack and bombardment by missiles is a strategic essential in preparation for the infantry to advance. In spiritual warfare intercession is what softens up the ground in order to prepare for the invasion. When we intercede, it's like we are sending projectiles which weaken the enemy, so that Satan loses strength, retreats, and takes his dirty hands off the city.

In physical warfare, a battle cannot be won by an air campaign alone. What is required is a landing and ground invasion involving hand to hand combat. In spiritual warfare, the ground offensive begins when the Church goes out into the streets to preach the Gospel in the open air, so that everyone can have the opportunity to hear the message of Jesus. Then no-one will be able to say that they haven't heard the good news of salvation. Not only do we pray, intercede, and fire off those spiritual missiles, but we also take the land as we advance from house to house and street to street preaching the Gospel.

During our evangelism campaigns there are two things that we do: In the air we wage spiritual warfare; and on the land we go village to village, city to city, preaching and giving testimony on TV and radio. We do both of these things at the same time. Through this approach, the Lord has blessed our ministry and we have seen thousands of people converted.

It's not sufficient to only labor in prayer; we must be willing to put legs on our prayers and go out and evangelize. If all we do is pray, we won't be very successful. Nor will we have success if we go out to evangelize without first engaging in the prayer battle so that the devil is forced to let go of the souls he has ensnared. Both of these things are necessary to achieve victory in the spiritual realm and see souls come running to the feet of Jesus. Spiritual warfare requires both intercession and preaching.

CHAPTER 3

Know Your Enemy

"Or suppose a king is about to go to war against another king. Won't he first sit down and consider whether he is able with ten-thousand men to oppose the one coming against him with twenty-thousand?" (Luke 4:31)

If an army intends to launch an attack, the first thing that they need to do is to understand exactly who they are facing and what sort of weapons their adversary is carrying. If it ignores the capability and armaments of the enemy, then the only thing that the army will achieve is to lose the battle. This is why so much money is invested in gathering intelligence, and failing to do this adequately is likely to prove very costly.

However, Christians often try to ignore the devil, thinking that by doing so they can escape attack, or perhaps they assume it is something they don't need to be concerned about. But he is our enemy, and we need to know what kind of weapons we are up against.

Our battle is against the devil and his army. He is our enemy! Surely that means that we can talk about him. He is a devil who has been defeated but the Church still needs to know certain things about him. What his goals are, why did he come, and what are his schemes?

No child of God should be afraid to talk about Satan's plans because he needs to be exposed. I have met quite a few people who are even afraid to mention his name, thinking that maybe if they ignore him then they will be out of his reach. The devil has been defeated! It was Jesus who defeated him, and we have been given authority by the Lord so that we can defeat the devil too. Believe me when I tell you that the devil is not going to respect us just because we ignore him.

The Word of God says in John 10:10 that the devil came, "... to steal, kill, and destroy." He is our enemy. His sole purpose on this earth is to completely disrupt and destroy God's children and God's creation.

Do Not Be Ignorant of the devil's Schemes

I am deeply struck by the fact that a large part of the Church does not want to hear mention of Satan. They even think, "Let's leave him alone so that he doesn't bother us." But I'm sorry to tell you that it doesn't work that way because there is no way that he is going to respect us. I believe it is a serious error to think that if we don't interfere with his plans, then he will not interfere with ours. The very purpose of his existence is to destroy us. The devil will always be committed to our destruction, no matter what our attitude is towards him.

There is a danger of two extremes. One is to glorify the devil and see demons everywhere; the other is just to ignore him. It is dangerous to believe that we are completely immune to his schemes, and that he cannot touch us. He cannot harm us if we remain rooted in the Word of God. That's why the Apostle Paul said that we need to be filled with the Holy Spirit and not give an opening to the devil, so that he cannot gain an entrance into our life, Ephesians 4:27 put it this way, "...and do not give the devil a foothold."

We need to live in holiness, being rooted in the Word of God because the devil is always ready to pounce and will get us when we drop our guard. One of his main weapons is to sow fear in the lives of those who are working to expose and confront him. But all those who are standing against him need to know that they have a God-given authority to dominate and command him in Jesus name. His schemes to frighten us take many forms and guises, but we need to remember that he is a liar who cannot ignore or disobey the authority of the name of Jesus.

BEELZEBUB IN THE TENT

I would like to tell you about something that happened on the first night of the evangelism campaign that we did a few years ago in a suburb of Buenos Aires called La Boca. The site of the campaign was just a few-hundred meters from the famous stadium of the Boca Juniors Football Club. We had trained about five-hundred volunteers to help us in the deliverance tent. At the end of the meeting, many people came forward to give their lives to Jesus. As we prayed with them for deliverance, many experienced demonic manifestations, and a huge number of people were taken to the deliverance tent to receive ministry.

Each evening of the campaign after the Gospel message, we give an altar call for those who would like to invite Jesus into their hearts. We then rebuke the devil, commanding him to loose the souls of those who have committed their lives to the Lord. After praying for healing, for the needs of those present, and for the baptism of the Holy Spirit, we come down from the platform to pray for each person who has come forward with the laying on of hands. There are usually several thousand people waiting to receive ministry.

This particular evening was no different. I was at the front, praying for people, when suddenly one of the volunteers, who was clearly upset, came running over from the deliverance tent shouting "Brother Carlos! Brother Carlos! Please come with me quickly!" My immediate response was to ask what had happened and why I had to go in person because I was busy praying for the many people who were waiting to receive ministry.

From her answer, I realized she was terrified! "It's Beelzebub! Beelzebub is in the deliverance tent!" The volunteer was trying to tell me that inside the deliverance tent was a person who was experiencing a fierce demonic manifestation and claiming to be Beelzebub.

He had a grotesque appearance, was roaring like a wild animal, and threatening all those around him and shouting, "I am Beelzebub!"

She said everyone was terrified, and some had even fled, fearing that they were about to be attacked. They were all asking me for help because no one had the courage to bind the spirit that was controlling the person. "Brother, you come and do it because you have the authority!" pleaded the volunteer who had called me, still distraught at what was happening. So I told her clearly "Sister. I am not going to do it, because it is not me who has the authority, but those who believe."

The Bible assures us in Mark 16:16-18 that these signs will accompany "those who believe." If we believe that we have the authority then no devil can stand against us. Not even the greatest of demons, or Satan himself, has authority to refuse or ignore an order given in the name of Jesus.

So I said, "Sister, go back to the tent and tell the volunteers with you to take authority and to command the spirit to leave in the name of Jesus." The volunteer went off and I continued praying for those gathered in front of the platform. After about ten minutes, I noticed the same volunteer shouting to be heard above the crowd. Only this time was different, and she wasn't asking for help. She ran up to me with her hands in the air, and I could make out a smile of victory on her face. "It works, Brother Carlos, it works!" she told me delightedly. "We bound Beelzebub in the name of Jesus, just as you told us, and then we commanded him to leave. The guy has been set free. Halleluiah!"

They had managed to bind the demon that was controlling that man. He had renounced all his sins, and then they had commanded the spirit of Beelzebub to leave in the name of Jesus.

THE ARMY OF SATAN

We also need to know that, in addition to reinforcing ignorance about his existence, which he uses effectively, the devil has a large army to help him in his fight against the children of God. Contrary to what many people think, Satan is not disorganized for he was taught according to the doctrine of the angels. We mustn't forget that he was second in command until he rebelled and was driven out of heaven. That means his army is like a structured military unit with levels of authority and various ranks that follow the orders of their superiors, completely respecting their authority.

The second part of Ephesians 6:12 shows us this hierarchy or command structure very clearly, "For we do not wrestle against flesh and blood, but against principalities, against powers, against the rulers of the darkness of this age, against spiritual *hosts* of wickedness in the heavenly *places.*" (NKJV)

Satan is fiercely opposed to the expansion of the Kingdom of God. He also has a kingdom—the kingdom of darkness. He is the absolute ruler or monarch of his kingdom as the following verses demonstrate: "...It is by the prince of demons that he drives out demons... " (Matthew 9:34) And reflecting an army of darkness the Scripture describes, "...a band of destroying angels..." (Psalm 78:49b) He also diligently tours his kingdom and its minions throughout the earth as Job illustrates, "The Lord said to Satan, 'Where have you come from?' Satan answered the Lord, 'From roaming throughout the earth, going to and fro on it.'" (Job 1:7) The Scripture also refers to him as the prince of this world, "...now the prince of this world will be driven out." (John 12:31b)

In this army there are principalities. The term principality is of Latin origin and means "Title or rank of a prince; territory or place in submission to the authority of a prince." It is the highest authority and level of government in a monarchic state. The prince or principality has power over a nation.

There are also powers. According to the Merriam-Webster dictionary, a power is: "a: possession of control, authority, or influence over others; b: one having such power; specifically: a sovereign state; c: a controlling group: establishment—often used in the phrase the powers that be."[1] What is the "authority, or influence over others" in this case? It is the power and governance

---

1. https://www.merriam-webster.com/dictionary/power

of the devil. Satan, the ruler, orders and directs all activities and operations within the area which has been assigned to him.

There are also rulers of the darkness of this age. The ruler or governor is the head of a province, region, or city, corresponding to a rank lower down the hierarchy than a power. This governor has authority within a defined area and rules according to the directives of the power or by royal proxy.

Then there are hosts. The hosts are groupings of soldiers in a military campaign. This term is used for those foot-soldiers who are fighting for the cause and who are sent to fight. When the above passage refers to hosts, it is not referring to a senior military rank. For the sake of our discussion, Satan's hosts appear to be formations of demons similar to what we would view as a brigade, division, or infantry unit. According to the Bible they are intelligent, but evil beings, without a physical body.

Clearly Satan has a strong, united, and vast body of armed forces.

THE ANGEL OF THE LORD DEFENDS US

One day, a woman who had been late leaving work, decided to take a taxi to get to her destination on time. "Where to?" asked the taxi driver.

"To the junction of Independence Street and Alvarado." "To the evangelism campaign?" asked the driver.

"Yes! Why do you ask? Have you already been there?" asked the woman.

"Yes, I've been along to watch," replied the driver, "but the guy who speaks seems a bit of a show-off."

"Oh. Why do you think that?"

"Well, can you tell me why the evangelist needs to have those five people dressed in white suits who walk across the stage while he's talking to the crowd?"

The taxi driver may not have realized it, but the Bible explains who the five people in white that he saw on the platform were.

According to Psalm 34:7 "The angel of the Lord encamps around those who fear him; and he delivers them." For this reason we don't need to be afraid of what the devil wants to do to us. Satan cannot touch a hair of our head. It is sin, and sin alone, that opens the door to the devil.

We've said that the thief comes to steal, kill, and destroy, and that we need to know our enemy. We do not need to be afraid of him, but we must take him seriously for he is always trying to create problems for us.

For example, do you know what the devil did during the first evangelism campaign that I held? He wanted to set my car on fire. I was preaching the Gospel and witches, spiritualists, and drug addicts were getting converted; every night, people came running from the street into the campaign site. That's why the devil was extremely upset—we were plundering his kingdom. So, to try and frighten me away, some people came to the campaign one day with the intention of turning over my car, and then spraying it with alcohol to set it on fire. They thought that if they did this, I wouldn't come back. At the time I was driving a Citroën. But much to their surprise, when they touched my car, they were immediately knocked flat on their backs by the Holy Spirit.

On another occasion, a group of people came to the campaign site early one morning and robbed all the chairs. The next day, when the meeting was about to start, one of the brothers came running up to me to say that the criminals who had stolen the chairs had just brought them all back. Evidently, every time they had tried to sit on one, they felt an intense heat that burned their backsides!

God is at work! The Holy Spirit of God is on the earth and His angels are here to help us. Sometimes when I am praying I beseech God asking, "Lord, send five-thousand legions of angels." People often wonder why I do this. Well, it's so that God can do the kind of things that I have been describing, and so the devil does not make us look stupid. Jesus himself, as he hung on the cross, assured us that if He wanted to, He could ask the Lord to send His angels and they would come to help immediately. Do we not have the same authority?!

Do you need help? Ask the Lord to send legions of angels and He will send them. If you are working in a tough neighborhood, then cry out to your God urging Him, "Lord, send your angels to help me evangelize this neighborhood." Then you will see that the Lord never lets us down.

I WILL GIVE YOU AUTHORITY

Often the devil comes to intimidate me and growls out threats like, "You can't get me!" Sometimes he crosses the platform while I am preaching or praying to shout at me that I can't touch him. My response is always the same, "I can't, but the One who is with me certainly can. Hallelujah! Satan get out, in the name of Jesus!"

This is the authority that God has given us to do His work. It's not that I'm especially brave, but each minute of my life I rely on God and trust in His Word that tells me in Luke 10:19 "I have given you authority to trample on snakes and scorpions and to overcome all the power of the enemy; nothing will harm you."

From the outset of my ministry, I have prayed against the work of witches, faith healers, those involved in the occult, and against all the different cults in Argentina. I remember how in one of our campaigns, a senior witch was converted. He told me that once he realized his work was drying up (because he was losing followers as they were converted in our campaigns), he decided to seek the help of other witches in order to wipe me out. The news about our campaigns had upset all those servants of Satan who embraced the kingdom of darkness. So he had contacted other witches in Brazil, Paraguay, Bolivia, and as far away as France, where witches were aware of the trouble we were causing them. So they had agreed together to use witchcraft in order to put me out of business.

But once this witch was converted, he immediately came to tell me what he had done. "Brother Carlos, the witches of Brazil,

Uruguay, Paraguay and Bolivia say that they are going to destroy you!" At that moment I felt a chill run down my spine from the top of my head to the tip of my toes—I was afraid. But immediately, I heard a voice in my ear telling me, "Carlos, I have given you authority to overcome all the work of the enemy, and nothing will harm you." Hallelujah! As 1 John 4:4 assures us, "You, dear children, are from God and have overcome them, because the one who is in you is greater than the one who is in the world."

CHAPTER 4

The Authority of Satan

1 Peter 5:8 admonishes us to, "Be alert and of sober mind. Your enemy the devil prowls around like a roaring lion looking for someone to devour." So we know that Satan never gives up trying to destroy us. Day and night he focuses all his energies on making our lives miserable. All his forces are working with the sole purpose of destroying God's creation—there is nothing more important to him.

The devil's work does not depend on whether we believe in him or not. In fact, the greatest deception of recent times lies in the widespread denial of the devil's existence. He is a liar and the father of lies, and denying his existence creates a great advantage for him. That is because when he is ignored, he has greater latitude and stealth to attack us. Ignoring him will not allow us to remain hidden or out of his line of sight. Furthermore, he shows no mercy so it doesn't matter to him if we try to ignore him. Even if we don't mention his name, he still prowls around like a roaring lion, looking for someone to devour.

I do not preach the devil; I preach Christ. I speak about the Lord, His love, His blessings. But when I teach, I teach about our enemy the devil. We need to know not only about the power that we have to confront the devil, but also about the authority that he has. And the exercise of our authority requires that we understand how the devil operates.

To Which Kingdom Do You Belong?

Let's look for a moment at what the Apostle John tells us in 1 John 5:19: "We know that we are children of God." He wants to open our eyes to the spiritual reality that we belong to God, who is with us; His angels are around us day and night to keep us safe. We know that we have been called by God, and that our lives are in His hands.

However, the above verse goes on to say, "...and that the whole world is under the control of the evil one." So we can conclude that many people belong to the Lord. But how many do not belong to the Him? Many, many more! Jesus expressed this very clearly in Matthew 12:30 when he said, "Whoever is not with me is against me, and whoever does not gather with me scatters." This is absolutely black and white, clear as crystal. There are no gray areas; there is one side or the other. We either belong to the kingdom of God or we belong to the kingdom of Satan.

I frequently hear people say things like, "He's not a Christian, but he's a good person." I am sorry to tell you that no matter how good a person may be, if they do not belong to Christ, then they are under the control of the evil one. We all sin, even good people! The famous whom we admire, kings and their subjects, governments and those whom they govern, astronauts, Nobel Prize winners, artists, and football players...

Those who come to Christ in faith and repentance, however, have their sins washed away and are reconciled to God through Jesus. Then they belong to the Lord and are part of His Kingdom. Sadly, however, those who have not made this decision remain under the control of the evil one. At some point the devil will use these people's lives because they belong to him; they are under his authority and he is their father.

So how important is all this? It is even more important than we can imagine. How much authority does the devil have that he can have the whole world under his feet? In order to understand this, we must explain it from the beginning.

WHAT THEN IS THE AUTHORITY OF SATAN?

The first part of the answer to this question is found in Luke 4: 5-8 which tells us, "The devil led him up to a high place and showed him in an instant all the kingdoms of the world. And he said to him, 'I will give you all their authority and splendor; it has been given to me, and I can give it to anyone I want to. If you worship me, it will all be yours.' Jesus answered, 'It is written: Worship the Lord your God and serve him only.'"

The first time I read this passage, it had a big impact on me. I could not understand what was written. It really troubled me. My main problem was with the devil's statement that "I will give you all their authority and splendor; it has been given to me, and I can give it to anyone I want to."

I immediately asked the Lord how it was possible that Satan could have so much authority unless God had given it to him. I couldn't understand who could have given him such a vast sphere of authority so that he could tell the Lord that he was the one who would decide to whom he would give the kingdoms and the authority over all the earth. Did all this really belong to Satan I wondered? How could the devil wield such authority?

I also noted that Jesus did not answer him by saying "You are lying!" Instead Jesus quoted the Word of God, saying "It is written: 'Worship the Lord your God and serve him only.'" I felt very confused, because I could not understand what authority Satan has on the earth.

As I searched for an answer, the Lord directed me to different passages of Scripture which speak of Satan as "the god of this age" and refer to "the powers of this dark world." Then I began to see that the Lord recognizes the devil has acquired this authority. I also realized that "all the kingdoms of the earth" means the whole world; all the nations of the world with no country excluded. It's really hard to understand the vast scope of authority that the devil has over all the nations of the earth. Many times it is easier to talk about other subjects, but it is important to understand what has really happened here.

As I became interested, I asked the Lord how it was that Satan had managed to get such authority, if it had not been granted to him by Jesus. I asked the Lord to give me understanding from His Word. I knew very well that it was not God who had given him such authority, because He made all the kingdoms of this earth for man and not for the devil. He created the earth and adorned it with all His splendor. Our minds cannot fathom the wonders of God's creation.

In the beginning, the earth was without form and empty, but God brought order by the work of His hands and filled what was empty. For what purpose? So that the devil; the thief and murderer could destroy the work of God's hands? No! God created the Earth for us and for our enjoyment. After He had finished adorning the Earth by creating trees, plants, flowers, birds, beasts of the field, and stunning landscapes, the Lord took the dust of the earth in His hands and made man. Then He set him as ruler over all creation, saying, "Be fruitful and increase in number; fill the earth and subdue it. Rule over the fish in the sea and the birds in the sky and over every living creature that moves on the ground." (Genesis 1:28)

The comparison that comes to mind is when parents prepare their home for the birthday of one of their children. They put up streamers and balloons, and decorate everything to make the child feel happy. God's love for us is so great that He has adorned the earth with breathtaking splendor and crowned it by placing us in the midst of it, saying "All this I have done for you to enjoy."

God did not create us to live broken lives full of problems, difficulties, bitterness, and sadness. I already understood this full well, but what I didn't understand was the one who gave authority over the nations of the earth to Satan.

GOD'S COVENANT WITH ADAM AND WITH NOAH

One day, God led me to read the following verse from the Book of Genesis. And as the Holy Spirit taught me, for the first time I understood the challenge that Satan gave to Jesus in the desert.

"God blessed them, and said to them (Adam and Eve), 'Be fruitful and increase in number; fill the earth and subdue it. Rule over the fish in the sea and the birds in the sky and over every living creature that moves on the ground." (Genesis 1: 28)

What was God doing with Adam and Eve? God was crowning mankind with a covenant. I can picture God taking Adam and Eve by the shoulder and walking with them in the light of day. God was giving them the keys and the title deed to the Earth. He commanded them to "subdue it" and "rule over" the wildlife, all of nature, and the ecology, meaning; *to take control of something, and give orders as its owner.*

In other words, God was saying to Adam and Eve, "You can do what you want, steward the Earth, manage it, and be masters of the creation." Nobody had more authority than them. They could do as they pleased, without having to ask or consult anyone. God gave complete authority and dominion of the Earth to Adam and Eve, saying, "Rule over it and subdue it."

Then in Genesis 9:1-2, we find another covenant which God made, this time with Noah and his sons as the Scripture tells us, "Then God blessed Noah and his sons, saying to them, 'Be fruitful and increase in number and fill the earth. The fear and dread of you will fall on all the beasts of the earth, and on all the birds in the sky, on every creature that moves along the ground, and on all the fish in the sea; they are given into your hands."

When we compare these two covenants, we see that there is a stark difference between them. It is a very important difference. The covenant that God made with Noah was not the same as the one that He made with Adam and Eve. In this new covenant the basic command to "subdue it" was not included. This shows that mankind no longer had the authority that they had been given in the beginning. What could be the reason for the difference? What had happened between the time that these two covenants were made?

The Crown Has Fallen From Our Heads

Something very important had happened, something that changed the whole course of human life and history. The reason for the difference is stated very clearly in Genesis Chapter 3, which describes the fall of mankind through rebellion and disobedience as Satan defeated Adam and Eve in the Garden of Eden. I can just picture Adam and Eve as they were being expelled from the Garden of Eden... Longingly looking back in desperation and seeing the cherubim with its sword drawn forever blocking their return.

That was the moment sin took hold of them. And that sin did much more than deprive mankind of life in Eden, where all was happy and they could walk with God Himself. In Lamentations 5:16 it is written, "The crown has fallen from our head. Woe to us, for we have sinned!" Satan triumphed because of the disobedience of mankind, snatching the keys and title deed to the earth, thus usurping the crown given to mankind. Through his disobedience to God, the first man handed to Satan what God had placed in his hands and trusted him with.

In the wars of old, when one king was triumphant in battle against another, it was not enough for him to simply be the victor. His victory meant much more than merely emerging the winner. Everything that had belonged to his opponent until then, passed legally into the hands of the victorious king. This included all their possessions, properties, and territories—they would all come under the authority of the victor. The people who were conquered lost all authority and in their subjugation were given into slavery and domination by a new kingdom.

Not only did mankind lose all that God had placed into their hands; through sin they became slaves of Satan, belonging to his kingdom. This was how the devil was able to come before Jesus in the desert and challenge Him by saying, "I will give you all their (the kingdoms of the earth) authority and splendor; it has been given to me."

Who then was guilty of surrendering authority over all the kingdoms of the earth to Satan? Mankind! We were guilty... Because of our disobedience, God's creation finds itself enslaved by sin, destruction, death, violence, drugs, promiscuity, and all sorts of darkness.

You might be wondering why I mention us, and not just Adam and Eve when I refer to who is responsible for this state of affairs. Well, there's a reason. Before I became a Christian, if someone told me about Adam and about sin, my immediate response was, "How am I to blame for what another man did? A man who had nothing to do with me, and who lived many thousands of years ago?" I believed that if God was good, then He would not hold me responsible for something that Adam did. That was my excuse, because I didn't know what was in the scriptures.

The Bible explains that the curse on God's creation is a result of Adam's sin. Because of the sin of one man, evil entered the world. It doesn't matter how good we are or try to be, we are each as guilty as Adam. Romans 5:12 describes it like this, "Therefore, just as sin entered the world through one man, and death through sin, and in this way death came to all people, because all sinned."

But praise God because that's not the end of the story, because the same passage of Scripture continues, "For if the many died by the trespass of the one man, how much more did God's grace and the gift that came by the grace of the one man, Jesus Christ, overflow to the many!" (Romans 5:15)

It is true that Satan won a legal right over mankind. He was not lying to Jesus when he tempted Him, nor had he taken by force what had belonged to Adam. No, it was given to him. He became master and owner of all that the Lord had made. But Jesus did what Adam could not do to recover what had been lost. He came to pay the debt that we all owed to God.

THE DEBT IS PAID

The day that Jesus Christ came into my life, I understood for the first time the immensity of what He did on the cross. On the 19th of May, 1979, my wife and I decided to give our lives to the

Lord. And as we shared that first prayer that completely changed our lives, with tears streaming down our faces, God showed me a vision… My hands were raised in surrender and commitment to Jesus, and I could see Him placing a piece of paper in my hands. It was a receipt on which was written, "Father, the debt that Carlos had with you is now settled. I've paid it." And below it was a name… It was signed by Jesus himself, but not in the same ink as the rest of the note. It was signed in His own blood, the blood of Jesus, shed on the cross of Calvary. Jesus settled the debt that we all had with God, and in the process took back all that mankind had lost.

CHAPTER 5

It is Finished

"When he had received the drink, Jesus said, 'It is finished.' With that, he bowed his head and gave up his spirit." (John 19:30)

There are no words in history overflowing with such power and victory as those that Jesus uttered seconds before giving up his life, "It is finished." Let me explain this a little bit more. When Jesus died on the cross of Calvary after having been exposed to public humiliation and having taken on himself the sins of us all, He made a visit to an unexpected place; He descended into hell itself.

In that dark place, Satan and all his company were engaged in a tremendous celebration that they believed would continue for eternity as they proclaimed, "We won! We have defeated the Son of God!" Death himself was ready to enslave Jesus for ever and ever. But great was his surprise, when at the very time he did not expect it, the gates of hell were suddenly wrenched open.

Nobody present at that party expected Jesus to arrive, for He was the very one that they had violently eliminated a few hours earlier. His death was the very reason they were celebrating. The demons had expected His appearance to be that of a slave to death, but when He entered, His steps were those of the King of kings and Lord of lords.

All hell froze before such authority. The party was over in a second. No one dared to utter even a single word or make any sound. Jesus, with His piercing gaze of absolute authority, stood facing death himself. And with the voice of one who emerges the victor in battle, He proclaimed these precious and unforgettable words, "Where, O death, is your victory? Where, O death, is your sting?" (1 Corinthians 15:55) The one who reigned and governed the kingdom of the dead had lost his authority.

The Bible tells us that the wages of sin is death. (Romans 6:23) But death could not hold Jesus, because He had no sin. Now He was defeating and humiliating hell in its entirety. Jesus, the conquering King, was stripping Satan of that which he had robbed from mankind at the beginning of creation, the keys and the title deed to the earth.

But that was not all. When He ascended from hell as the victorious King, having accomplished His mission, He displayed to all heaven what He was carrying in his hands! In His left hand were the keys and title deed to the Earth; in His right hand, reconciliation between God and mankind. Hallelujah! Jesus recovered what mankind had lost in the Garden of Eden.

THE SCALE OF THE REDEMPTIVE WORK OF JESUS

What I have just related enables us to understand clearly the significance of what Jesus did that precious day on the cross of Calvary. The Bible tells us in 1 Corinthians 15:22, "For as in Adam all die, so in Christ all will be made alive." Jesus reversed the condition of mankind. From the time of Adam till the day when Jesus gave up His life, mankind was in bondage to Satan because of sin.

After being expelled from the Garden of Eden, mankind lost all its privileges. And the greatest privilege of them all was walking with God. After sinning, there was no possibility for humans to enter into the presence of God, except through sacrifices. Satan made sure to rob Adam of something he knew was the key to living a life full of peace and happiness; having communion with God, by walking together with Him and talking face to face with his Creator.

From this we can see the value of what Jesus won back for us. He raised us to our original status. His sacrifice restored to us the incredible privilege of being able to walk again with God, at all times and in all places, just as Adam and Eve did in the beginning.

We need to grasp this truth, *God is with us!* There are no longer any barriers that separate us from Him. There are no impediments, and nothing and nobody can hinder our fellowship with God. We can talk to Him any time and any place. We can rely on Him wherever we are. Jesus took away all that separated us from God. Now, through Jesus, the way is open for all. Let's enter in by this way to live a victorious life.

THE AUTHORITY OF THE CHURCH

One of the wonderful things that Jesus took back from the devil, made possible by His sacrifice on the Cross, is the authority that had been stolen. That authority now belongs to the Church. All who believe, who are children of God, and who walk hand in hand together with Him, are the rightful owners of this precious authority. Jesus recovered what we had lost because of our sin, and entrusted it to His Church.

The authority that the Church, the body of Christ, has received is much greater than we can imagine. Not even hell itself can stand against it. This was what Jesus said in Matthew 16:18, "And I tell you that you are Peter, and on this rock I will build my church, and the gates of Hades will not overcome it."

In the unity of the body of Christ is found the highest authority to overcome the kingdom of darkness. By praying in agreement, we can dominate any spiritual force in the spiritual realm that is affecting the physical world, and place it in subjection. We have authority to bind the devil and all his cohorts, and to release the abundant blessings and wonders of God on our lives. Jesus assured us of this when He declared, "Truly I tell you, whatever you bind on earth will be bound in heaven, and whatever you loose on earth will be loosed in heaven. Again, truly I tell you that if two of you on earth agree about anything they ask for, it will be done for them by my Father in heaven. For where two or three gather in my name, there am I with them." (Matthew 18: 18-20)

As the Church of Jesus Christ, we must believe that there are no limits to the exercise of this authority. Those who are children of God by faith need to take hold of it in order to live a life of victory. Those of us who believe, and who live according to the will of God and what His Word teaches, have authority to overcome temptation and to defeat the devil in all areas of our lives. That applies to our marriage, among our children, at work, in our studies, with our health, and more... We can live a life of complete victory. As James 4:7 instructs us, "Submit yourselves, then, to God. Resist the devil, and he will flee from you."

So then, we know that we have received spiritual authority, which should be reflected first in our lives. But, as with all things of God, what we have received is not only for personal benefit. As children of God we have a responsibility. Everyone needs to ask themselves the following question, "What is the purpose of this authority that I have received? What is my responsibility as a child of God?"

THE PURPOSE OF THE AUTHORITY WE HAVE

The Lord has anointed us, and given us an authority which comes with a purpose. The Bible clearly states in the Book of Isaiah that this is for preaching the good news, binding up the wounded, and proclaiming freedom to the captives. "The Spirit of the Sovereign Lord is on me, because the Lord has anointed me to proclaim good news to the poor. He has sent me to bind up the broken-hearted, to proclaim freedom for the captives and release from darkness for the prisoners." (Isaiah 61:1)

On various occasions, Jesus showed us that we have authority, and He also taught us what we should use it for. When He commissioned the twelve disciples, He told them, "Heal those who are ill, raise the dead, cleanse those who have leprosy, drive out demons. Freely you have received; freely give." (Matthew 10:8)

And in Luke 10:19, Jesus instructed the seventy-two He sent out as follows, "I have given you authority to trample on snakes and scorpions and to overcome all the power of the enemy; nothing will harm you."

Then there is the most important of all the commands that Jesus gave us which we have come to know as the Great Commission. It summarizes the authority that Jesus has given us, "He said to them, 'Go into all the world and preach the gospel to all creation. Whoever believes and is baptized will be saved, but whoever does not believe will be condemned. And these signs will accompany those who believe: in my name they will drive out demons; they will speak in new tongues; they will pick up snakes with their hands; and when they drink deadly poison, it will not hurt them at all; they will place their hands on people who are ill, and they will get well.'" (Mark 16: 15-18) Jesus gave us this authority so that we could exercise it on behalf of the needy.

AUTHORITY NEEDS TO BE TESTED

One morning, as I was reading the newspaper, I came across a report about a town in Patagonia in the south of Argentina. It was about the city of Las Heras, in the province of Santa Cruz. This small town has a population of about nine-thousand. It is a very cold place, with strong winds and a semi-desert climate. It's not a place for tourists and the only people who live there are workers in the oil industry. At that time there was a confrontation between a group of oil workers and the town council. Things came to a head with a man who was killed in a clash between an armed group and the local police.

As I read this distressing news, God spoke to me about visiting the town to do an evangelism campaign as soon as possible. We immediately got in touch with the churches and the pastors of the region. After discussions with them about the situation, we made arrangements to hold a campaign. The town council was helpful and offered us a hall to hold our meetings.

God did powerful miracles and many were healed. Members of the town council also came along to hear the message about Jesus. As the Holy Spirit touched people's hearts, we watched as those who had been trying to kill each other just a few days before were reconciled to each other. Most of the people of the town came to our meetings, and there was a wonderful atmosphere of peace.

I remember very clearly something that happened on the third night of the four-day campaign. After the message, we had given the altar call, prayed for deliverance and for the sick, and then listened to some of the wonderful testimonies. I came down from the platform to minister to those who had come forward, when suddenly I was confronted with a terrible sight. Waiting in line with the others, was a giant of a man of about thirty-years of age. When I went to pray for him, he grunted in a grotesque voice, "What have you come to do?"

The Holy Spirit showed me that it was the strong man of that city who was speaking to me. He was not pleased with what we were doing, and had come to stop us. Immediately I could feel my body start to tremble. Although I was standing still, the muscles in my face were twitching, and my arms and legs were shaking. It was the first time I had experienced such a situation. However, at no time did fear take over. I understood that the demonic presence in that man was so strong that it was causing all my muscles to shake.

Immediately, I raised my head to look into his eyes. In that instance, for the first time in my life, I saw the very face of Satan. Those who were around me had the same experience. The man reacted by taking about ten paces backwards, leaving me alone with a few helpers, who were waiting for me to tell them what to do. Then I went up to the spirit and gave the command, "Satan, in the name of Jesus, I bind you!" With the authority of the Lord, I then ordered the man to lower his arms, which were raised and poised ready to strangle me. He remained immobile, in the position in which I had bound him, with his hands by his sides, but he continued to roar and shake.

I left him like that and went on with the task of praying for the other people gathered at the altar. During all this time the man stood motionless, waiting for the next order that I would give. I observed many strange things as he waited. Some moved away from him, fearing that perhaps the devil would attack them. Others, including pastors, did not dare go near him, for fear that the spirit might leave the man and seize them. But from my experience of ministering deliverance over thirty-years, I can assure you that there is no way that could happen. Never ever have we had the experience of seeing a demon exit one person and then enter another. So no one needs to be afraid that this could happen. Sin is the only key that Satan has to open the door to a person's life.

During that half-hour, everyone was able to see that even the strong man of city, with various principalities under his control, had to submit and could do nothing but obey the commands given him in the name of Jesus. My message that night had referred to the authority the children of God have over the kingdom of darkness. God had illustrated my preaching through what had happened.

When I finished praying for all the people who were waiting, I went over to the man once again and gave the following order to the devil, "Satan, in the name of Jesus, I command you to leave this person, right now!"

Instantly, he collapsed heavily to the ground and then opened his eyes. He gave a big smile of relief and freedom. Standing to his feet with his hands held high, he gave glory to God—Satan had let him go! Hallelujah!

Through this experience, God gave me another lesson. The authority of His children will be tested, so they demonstrate that they believe in what has been entrusted to them. The story would not have ended well if I had not believed that I had authority in the name of Jesus. That man, who was under the influence of the devil, would probably have beaten me black and blue. But what I realized very clearly at the time, was that I had authority. It was not a human authority, but empowerment given me in the name of Jesus, and without which I would not have been able to confront that spirit. And this same authority has been given to the Church by Jesus Christ. If you believe, then you too have this authority.

The people who minister in the deliverance tent are not Christian leaders, pastors, or people with a special calling or gifting. They are members of the churches which have come together to organize the campaign. We teach them the meaning of authority. I can assure you that by the time each campaign ends, each one of them has proved that this authority is effective, because the Lord gives authority to those who believe, irrespective of their age or title. I can attest to this, because when I had been a Christian for only a few months, and knowing very little, I believed God and things started to happen. All I had was faith but that was enough for the authority of God to operate, and the signs began to appear.

AUTHORITY IS FOR ALL WHO BELIEVE

Contrary to what many people think, spiritual authority is not something unique to a person. It's not a special gift or ministry. Nor is it something extraordinary and supernatural that we only see on special occasions. Jesus has made it possible for every believer to experience His authority all the days of their lives. And authority is something that should be part of everyday life, to be used as and when it is necessary.

You need to know that you have authority in order to confront the kingdom of darkness, which is governed and nourished by the devil and all his forces. This is what happens when we believe and take authority in the name of Jesus.

Many ask me if deliverance is a specific ministry. Jesus didn't teach that. He said in Mark 16:17, "And these signs will accompany those who believe: in my name they will drive out demons;" There are no limits; for all who believe, trust, and are seeking God's perfect will for their lives, have power and authority. Obviously, there are certain conditions. We cannot live according to our own way of thinking without consulting the will of God, and pretend to exercise dominion over the spiritual world. The Bible teaches us how we should live and behave in order to have authority. And no one can have it, unless they first put themselves under that authority.

If we live under authority, Satan has to submit to our commands. However, if there is sin in our lives, what authority can we expect to have to overcome the devil? We have to be careful otherwise the same thing could happen to us that happened to the seven sons of Sceva, in Acts 19:13-16. The demons will not respect our commands, and they are the ones who will exercise authority over our lives!

FROM PRIESTESS OF DARKNESS TO SERVANT OF JESUS

I remember one night ministering at an evangelism campaign that was taking place close to an area where there was a lot of witchcraft, magic, spiritualism, Voodoo, and all kinds of occult activity. That evening, a woman of grotesque appearance came forward to receive ministry. I noticed that there was no hair on her head, which was covered with a scarf. As soon as she approached me, and before I had time to lay hands on her, she began to shake angrily.

Immediately, two of the volunteers who were at my side saw her fierce advance towards me and tried to restrain her. When I took authority over the spirit that was controlling the woman, the two volunteers put their arms around me to push me back, thinking that in this way they could save me from being attacked.

Over the years, however, God has taught me that spiritual authority does not work this way. As one person takes authority, the others need to keep still not talking or interfering. When a person experiences a demonic manifestation during a church service, it can often happen that those who are standing nearby start to pray, shout, and rebuke the spirits. But the devil doesn't obey any of them because he respects authority. When a situation like this occurs, deliverance becomes ineffective because each person inadvertently takes away the other's authority.

Then, while the volunteers were trying to defend me, the woman gave me a slap and her fingernails just caught the edge of my lips. I had to ask the volunteers to let me go because I didn't need any form of protection. I knew full well that in the name of Jesus, the devil cannot touch even a single hair of my head. So I went up to the woman and bound the spirit in the name of Jesus.

Just then, the Holy Spirit showed me that she was a witch. So I leaned over and spoke into her ear, "In the name of Jesus, if you do not repent now, then this will be the last day of your life, because God will take you." As I said those words, the woman fell to the ground, as though she had been struck down. My next thought was, "Lord, how can it happen so quickly?" She was then carried off to the deliverance tent by four volunteers and I lost track of her.

If someone experiences a demonic manifestation during one of our campaigns, the ushers accompany the person to the deliverance area, usually a tent. We do not attempt to minister to the person in public because it is important to respect a person's privacy and not expose them to the embarrassment of being observed. In the privacy of the tent, the person can confess and renounce the sins that have kept them bound, and so find deliverance.

This woman had a lot to confess because she was a high- level witch. Having made many demonic covenants, she had a large group of personal followers and spent several hours in the tent receiving ministry. After the campaign I heard nothing more from her and wondered how it turned out.

Much to my surprise, the next time we organized a campaign in the area, a well-dressed, elegant woman came forward to give testimony, this time sporting a full head of hair. Although she had been transformed completely, I still recognized her as the woman who had confronted me that night. She told the crowds that on the same night that she was touched by the Holy Spirit and set free from the demonic bonds in her life, she was healed of a disease that had been eating away at her life. She had been suffering from cancer but God in His mercy gave her a second chance and turned her into a new woman. He set her free from all the chains, sadness, and bitterness that had dominated her life, and healed her of that terrible disease.

In the deliverance tent, she had renounced all the demonic covenants she had made and occult practices that she had been involved in. She had promised Jesus that from that day forth she would no longer be a priestess of the devil, but a servant of Jesus Christ.

AUTHORITY FOR DELIVERANCE

God has given us the same power that He gave to the twelve disciples and to the seventy-two that Jesus sent out. What should we do while all the time the sick are dying, the devil is destroying families, and people are committing suicide? How sad it would be if God did not break the bonds that keep people bound, oppressed, and under the control of the devil, with no one to do anything for them. But thanks be to God that Jesus Christ, who has compassion for all those who suffer, has given us authority and power, and assured us, "These signs will follow those who believe: In My name they will drive out the demons that oppress, that keep people bound, and which destroy the lives of those He has created"

God will create opportunities for us to give what we have received and put it into practice. We also have the power to drive out demons, and to exercise authority over the spiritual world. So we need to be wise, and live lives worthy of the Lord, using the authority He has given us to do His will.

CHAPTER 6

The Gospel Unveiled

SATAN'S HEADQUARTERS

The following conversation has been adapted from the book "Passion for Souls" by Oswald Smith.

One evening, the rulers of the different regions met at Satan's headquarters to give an update on developments in the territories under their control. "Right, what's the news?" Satan asked, as he lifted his head and stared questioningly at the assembled group.

"Good news, sir!" replied the ruler of Region One. "They have been unable to achieve their aim."

"So they tried then?" responded Satan, as he looked into the face of the fallen angel.

"Yes, my Lord, but to no avail. All their efforts were frustrated." responded the ruler as he bowed, looking very pleased at his recent victory.

"So how did it go? Did you have a lot of work? Tell me all about it!" demanded Satan, keen to know more.

"Well," began the ruler, "As I was wandering through the territory under my command, I overheard a pastor saying that they were about to hold a meeting for all the pastors in the city to discuss the possibility of arranging an evangelism campaign.

"Just tell me what you did," Satan interrupted, impatient to hear the end of the story.

"Firstly, I called together all the forces of darkness under my command for a meeting. They made many suggestions, but we finally agreed that the best scheme was to prevent them from working together. That was really easy to do. All we had to do was to remind the pastors that some of those coming to the meeting had split away from existing congregations. We sowed feelings of bitterness and resentment. But that's not all. We also brought to light some sins from the past, thanks to critical comments about the pastors that we picked up from church members when they changed from one congregation to another. We sowed plenty of thoughts of jealousy and envy. With others, we used an even simpler strategy. All we had to do was remind them that they there were some doctrinal differences between the various pastors who had gathered. It was quite simple to make them lose sight of their objective. Finally, all we had to do was release among them a spirit of strife and division. That was the finishing touch that ended any plan of working together. Now they are more divided than ever. Our work was a complete success. I can say that everything is in order in my territory."

"Excellent! Great work! You have done me a great service," said the fallen cherub, with an expression of satisfaction on his face, which once had been beautiful.

Shouts and applause echoed through that dark and dreadful place.

"Continue your good work, ruler of Region One. Keep killing and destroying everything in your path, including the youth, marriages, the elderly, and children. Keep using drugs, alcohol, sex, and violence to ruin the region under your control. It looks like you should have no problems."

Then he turned to the ruler of the Region Two and enquired, "Well, what have you to report?"

"I've also got some great news that will make your Majesty really happy," said the ruler.

"Oh. Has there been an attempt to invade your region?" Satan asked, with growing interest.

"Indeed there was," replied the ruler. "I was carrying out my duties in the territory under my command, a region where there are very few churches. I was busy destroying congregations, dividing them, preventing the raising up of new servants of that unmentionable person (Jesus), when I heard the news that some new missionaries were going to be coming to my region from another country. I quickly called a meeting of the forces under my command and we soon came up with a plan, which we carried out with great success. We sent a strong spirit of sickness to oppress the missionaries. They soon gave up their call, thinking that they had made a mistake, and that perhaps preaching the Gospel was not so important after all."

"And that is not all, my Lord," continued the ruler. "We used people under our control to drive up the rental costs of the buildings where Christians have been meeting. Now they have decided to leave our area for good." As he concluded his report, a great shout of joy went from the assembled rulers who bowed before the majestic figure of Satan.

"And what have you got to report?" he asked, turning to another fallen angel. "Are you still the master of Region Three?"

"I'm afraid that my news is not good, my Lord," responded the ruler, slowly, without looking up to reveal the look of terror etched in his face.

"What!" thundered Satan, barely able to control himself. "Have you not been able to keep your region under control?"

"We did our best, your Majesty, but to no avail."

"Are you so useless that you couldn't even stop an evangelism campaign?" roared the boss, violently enraged. "Not only were our attempts to stop it unsuccessful, but the campaign went on for longer than scheduled. They've been preaching the Gospel every night for forty-days. Thousands have heard the message and many have been healed. My Lord, it's a disaster! There are even pastors and entire congregations coming to help from other areas. Even our supporters, the witches, are being converted. Your majesty, it's a complete failure."

"But that's not possible! I sent entire legions to support your efforts and you still couldn't stop it?!" bellowed Satan.

He then broke into an uncontrollable rage. The air was filled with millions of spirits. Their rulers were seated in front of Satan, terrified, as they struggled to avoid his piercing gaze. The entire assembly sat in rapt attention. Then the ruler stepped slowly forward, crestfallen, until he stood trembling before his sovereign.

"There was no way that we could stop them. Our forces worked day and night trying to beat them, but the heavenly army was more numerous than ours. Their Father sent many legions of angels to protect them and defeated us on all fronts. It seems they have started an organization whose sole purpose is evangelizing. The whole church has begun to pray and intercede. They are attacking us day and night with their prayer chains and fasting. The bombing and warfare are intense. They all seem to be aware that Christ will not come to reign unless the Gospel is preached in every nation and to people of all languages."

"We are fighting continually, but we can't stop them. They just keep advancing," he continued in a trembling voice.

"What are we going to do?" roared Satan. "All is lost! Thousands have been saved, and this last piece of news is the worst of all. He could come at any time. It will not be long, because with the vision that these people have, soon people of every tribe, language, and nation will be reached with the Gospel. And then what will become of me? Woe is me!"

THE RESPONSIBILITY OF THE CHURCH

One day, as I was interceding, God gave me a vision. I found myself in a beautiful place. There was lush green grass sprinkled with flowers and plants of all colours and shapes. I had never seen anything like it. I also saw a crowd of smiling, happy people who were enjoying that breathtaking panorama. I thought I must be in heaven.

But suddenly towards the back of this gorgeous countryside, I noticed a very high fence that was impossible to climb over. I wondered what it was, so in my vision, I went closer to the fence and looked over it. To my surprise, everything on the other side was brown and arid, with no vegetation—just lifeless. I could also make out shadows, and as I looked closer, I realized that it was inhabited by people who had been living for many years in this desert. Their clothes were worn, their hair was matted and messy, and they were gasping for something to drink.

Everyone was desperately staring at the oasis that was located on the side where I was standing, along with other believers. Some seemed to be holding out their hands for help, others were crawling, but all of them seemed to be asking for something. All I could make out were the words, "Help us! Give us some water, please!" They were trying to reach those of us who were on the other side, but there was no way we could span the barrier and reach them, nor could they crossover to us.

Then, all of a sudden, I sensed a voice urging me, "Tell my Church to take down every barrier, every fence, and all obstacles that separate them from those who hunger and thirst, not for bread and water, but for God."

That is the responsibility of the Church! Our responsibility is to ensure that the world has the opportunity to know Jesus Christ. If we want to win the lost, we need to advance on Satan's beachhead—move forward and fight in enemy territory because the world is under the control of the evil one. We know that we belong to God, and if we love people, we have to go into the devil's territory, into the world, and rescue the souls that Satan has enslaved. God has sent us to take back what the devil has stolen, but we must understand that we cannot enter the devil's territory empty handed! We must take the weapons that are required to win the battle.

HARDNESS OF HEART

Many times we make excuses insisting that people do not get converted because of the hardness of their hearts. But that is not the case. I remember one time when I was in Europe I got talking to a group of pastors. During the conversation, one of them commented, "Evangelism is hard going here because the people of this city are hard-hearted." I didn't respond, but the words stayed with me.

We were staying in a beautiful place near the sea and from the site of our campaign we could see some lovely properties. Some of them were mansions of three, four, or even five floors. I'm sure that those who lived there were upper class people who enjoyed great privilege and a lot of money.

As I admired the beauty and drank in the breathtaking view, God spoke to me, saying, "Carlos, go and knock on the door of one of those houses, and tell them you want to talk to them about me. They will listen to you." Suddenly, I understood the passage of Scripture that admonishes us with the words, "How, then, can they call on the one they have not believed in? And how can they believe in the one of whom they have not heard? And how can they hear without someone preaching to them?" (Romans 10:14) If we are afraid to speak, we will never be able to evangelize the entire world.

I preached in that city for nine nights in a huge tent with the capacity to hold eight-to-nine-thousand people. And to the surprise of many, it was filled every night of the campaign. Those who had said we could not evangelize because of the hardness of people's hearts watched wide-eyed with wonder as roughly two-thousand people came forward each evening with their hands held high surrendering their lives to Jesus.

THE VEILED GOSPEL

The task of evangelism depends on us, not on the people who need to hear it. 2 Corinthians 4:3-4 explains, "And even if our gospel is veiled, it is veiled to those who are perishing. The god of this age has blinded the minds of unbelievers, so that they cannot see the light of the gospel that displays the glory of Christ, who is the image of God."

Why is the Gospel veiled? It is because the god of this age, the thief, the usurper, has blinded the minds and the understanding of unbelievers so that they cannot see the light of the Gospel. There is no such thing as a heart that is hard towards God. Instead, Satan uses a spirit of unbelief to blind people's minds and understanding. If people don't believe, it's because a spirit of unbelief is controlling them.

So if our Gospel is veiled, and the god of this age has blinded the minds of unbelievers, what do we need to do to bring people to believe? We need to drive the god of this age out of the area and command him, "Satan, spirit of unbelief, loose the minds!" When Satan lets go of the minds, the light of the Gospel can shine in people's lives.

I always enjoy going to preach in homes. When I am able, or when I am invited to pray for someone in their home, I preach to all the members of the family. If they do not receive Jesus into their hearts, I don't pray for healing. But if they do receive Him, I ask the Lord to do a miracle. I'm not some sort of faith healer so the first thing I always do is preach the Gospel.

I have met all kinds of people. Once, when I was visiting a family, I began to speak about the Lord and all the members of the family sat around me listening carefully. The one exception was the grandmother, who stayed in the kitchen from where she could hear what was going on. Everyone seemed to be agreeing with what I was sharing except the grandmother who kept coming out of the kitchen to interrupt me. "You make people pay tithes," she protested.

Surprised by her comments, which had nothing to do with what I had been sharing, and trying not to lose the thread of what I was saying, I answered her, "No, ma'am, it's not like that. Don't get me wrong…" and then I tried to explain the matter to her. "I see," she said and retreated back to the kitchen.

No sooner had I gotten back to what I wanted to say to those around me, who were all listening intently, than the grandmother appeared again from the kitchen. "But you don't believe in Mary," she again interjected.

Once again I explained to her that while we believe in Mary and we love her, we don't venerate her because she is not God. Jesus is the one we worship.

By this time I was getting quite annoyed because every time those in the family were ready to make a commitment to Jesus, she would interrupt me and stop what we were doing. So I decided to ask if I could use the bathroom. And what did I do there? I got down on my knees and took authority, "Satan, spirit of unbelief, spirit of argument, loose the minds right now!"

I kept praying like this for several minutes. The place was a bit cramped for engaging the enemy in spiritual warfare and after a few minutes I could feel myself sweating. I came out of the bathroom red in the face and the assembled group looked on amused as I retook my place in the lounge.

This time, when the grandmother appeared, she took a seat beside me and said, "Pastor, it's lovely that you could join us today. Please go on with what you were saying." In the end, the whole family accepted Jesus—including the grandmother.

Remember that our struggle is not against flesh and blood; our enemies are the principalities and powers. We have power and authority in the name of Jesus, but Satan will only respect that authority when we exercise it. He no longer has rights over us, but he doesn't want to release that which he has held for so long without a struggle.

We exercise our authority as we stand in the authority of the name of Jesus and command Satan to release the souls that he has kept captive, and which do not belong to him. Then the power struggle begins! We have victory in our hands, but the devil does not want to admit it because he is a liar, a thief and a scoundrel. Don't give up; you have to expect him to fight to keep hold of the souls Jesus died for. That's why it's important to know what authority God has given us, how to use it, and what weapons we have to fight with.

THE WORKS OF SATAN

In 1985 the entire city of Rosario (located in central Argentina) was touched by the power of the Gospel. We saw thousands and thousands of people give their lives to Jesus. Most of the churches in the city were actively involved in the campaign. Denominational differences were laid aside as everyone joined together in order to win the lost for Christ. God responded by doing amazing miracles.

What I am about to relate, however, happened ten-years later, when I returned to Rosario to hold another evangelism campaign. One day, after our team intercession time, I headed into the center of the city to do some shopping. It was a day like any other; sunny, warm, and the forecast was good. Suddenly, as I walked along, I noticed litter flying around and the leaves on the trees starting to shake as a strange wind began to blow. I could see a blue sky above, so I couldn't understand why this sudden storm arose. The violent wind kept blowing, however, leading me to realize that something unusual was happening.

Rosario is nestled in the Province of Santa Fe, to the north of the city of Buenos Aires. As I watched this strange weather, I recognized that the wind was coming from the south. The dark clouds were coming from the direction of Buenos Aires, and they were coming together at different heights directly above the city where we were doing our campaign. Within a few seconds, the clouds had completely covered the city, blocking out the sun, and bringing with them this strange wind.

As I surveyed the scene, I heard God's voice saying, "Carlos, what you seeing are legions of demons, coming from Buenos Aires to oppose the campaign." The spiritual struggle was being made manifest before my eyes! I was watching the devil's preparations and schemes to ensure that the Gospel would not be preached. I realized that the spiritual rulers of the territory of Rosario were being reinforced by others from the province of Buenos Aires.

Satan was getting ready to withstand the campaign in order to prevent thousands of souls from coming to the feet of Jesus. This is why I never get tired of saying that the Bible is very clear when it says that our struggle is not against flesh and blood, but against the principalities, against powers, against the rulers of the darkness of this age, against spiritual *hosts* of wickedness in the heavenly places. This experience confirmed to me the importance of fighting and waging spiritual warfare to oppose the enemy as he tries to try to stop the advance of the Gospel.

SEIZING SOULS FROM THE DEVIL'S CLUTCHES

We cannot ask the Lord to do our work for us, and then sit around and wait for things to happen. He has granted us authority that we might use it to command the devil to free captive souls in the name of Jesus. As children of God, let us reclaim each of our cities and our nation for Christ, but let's realize that we need to fight for them.

The devil will not let go of anything without a fight, he will not just give us anything. We'll have to fight for everything in the name of Jesus. Do we want the city? Then we have to command him, "Satan loose the city, in the name of Jesus!" This is the only way to conquer him, by storming the gates of hell (Matthew 16:18).

How we pray will determine whether the powers and principalities will start to weaken and lose their grip—then we will see people running to the feet of Jesus. When the spiritual world starts to retreat in disarray, it doesn't matter who we are preaching to; their social status, or their culture, because they are no longer being controlled.

If you want to see your city transformed by the light of the Gospel, you need to take authority and fight in prayer and intercession against the devil and his forces, against the spirit of unbelief. You must order him to loose the lost, the minds he has blinded in the name of Jesus, then we can preach the Gospel, and people will respond.

When the pastors in a given city join together to organize an evangelism campaign, all hell is let loose. The principality over that particular municipality, with all his powers and forces, begins to put obstacles in place to try and stop the event. What I told you at the start of this chapter makes this very clear.

A City Transformed by the Power of God

In 1984, at the beginning of our ministry, we were preparing for a campaign in the city of Mar del Plata. We had planned the event to run some fifteen-days with the possibility of extending to twenty-days. When we arrived at this seaside resort on the coast of the province of Buenos Aires, we checked into a hotel located right on the seashore. At that time, Mar del Plata was the most important tourist city on the Atlantic Coast of Argentina. Between two-and-three hundred thousand people used to visit it each summer.

While one of my colleagues was filling in the forms at the reception desk, I went over to a large window to enjoy the view. Suddenly, a woman who had been leaning against one of the pillars which adorned the hotel lobby walked rapidly towards me and grabbed me by the arm. "Please tell me about Jesus," she implored me...

I was quite taken aback because I had never seen her before in my life. It was the first time that we were doing a campaign in this city, so she knew absolutely nothing about us or what we were doing there. So what was making her act in this strange way? We realized that the Holy Spirit was convicting her of her sins. That very day she had contemplated suicide because she felt overwhelmed by the problems in her life and unable to carry on. I didn't know her situation, but I could see the desperation etched in her face as she came over to ask me to tell her about Jesus. So I explained the Gospel to her, and with tears in her eyes, she accepted Jesus into her heart. She was the first person to get saved in that amazing 1984 campaign.

Still in a state of shock from what had just happened, I joined the others and we went up to our rooms. We entered the room that we were sharing, and my colleague went over to the window overlooking the sea. I could tell from his demeanor that he was receiving a vision and he started to tell me what he could see. He was amazed to see three giants rising over the sea trying to seize control of the city, but something like a huge invisible wall was stopping them. Around these giants were countless demons jumping on the water, rushing against the huge wall that held them back and bouncing off of it. I was amazed by the vision, and it was quite some time before my colleague recovered.

Once the campaign started, we realized the significance of the vision. One of the special things about the campaign was that all the churches of the city were taking part including: Mennonites, Brethren, Baptist, Christian Alliance, Pentecostals, Brethren, Assembly of God, Missionary Movement of Christ, and the Salvation Army. All these denominations, which rarely come together, were working alongside each other with the common goal of evangelizing the city of Mar del Plata.

Right from the start of the campaign, supernatural things began to happen. Some people were falling down in the streets under the influence of the Holy Spirit, others were experiencing demonic manifestations in their homes—the miraculous was everywhere. When we realized the incredible move of God that was taking place, we decided to extend the meetings. After we had been preaching for forty-five nights, we had to move to the main football stadium for an additional fifteen-days to accommodate all the people who wanted to attend.

In total, 83,054 people accepted Jesus as their Lord and Savior during that huge campaign entitled "Mar del Plat, Jesus Loves You!" in 1984. The largest, most widespread national newspapers and magazines carried headlines like "More People Attend Evangelical Meeting Than All Theatres and Events Combined." In the city stadium, the fans started to chant our campaign song, "The Man of Galilee," during Soccer matches.

The miracles that were taking place kept increasing and included many having their dental cavities filled with gold sent from heaven! So what was behind this great move of God and the supernatural outpouring of His grace? I attribute it to two dynamics, first, spiritual warfare and intercession, and second, the unity among the churches. We were able to see how, through these efforts, the strong man was kept bound and could not enter the city.

This clearly shows us the power of intercession, and that what Jesus prayed us in John 17:21is true, "...that all of them may be one, Father, just as you are in me and I am in you. May they also be in us so that the world may believe that you have sent me."

If we want to defeat the one who came to steal, kill, and destroy, then we as the Church, as the body of Christ, cannot stop praying, interceding, and doing spiritual warfare. When the strong man loses his authority, when the prince is bound, when the rulers are cast down, people begin to believe. Automatically, the god of this age loses his authority, he lets go of the minds of the people, and the Gospel shines out. That's why our struggle is not against flesh and blood. The Church has power and authority, and we must use it.

VICTORY IS IN OUR HANDS

We need to prepare our hearts to look at the crowds and declare, "Jesus loves you!" God has compassion for our land and for our people. Let us not back up even a single step, because we have already retreated too far. Satan has taken over the territory that we have left empty and unoccupied. We have abandoned the parks, the squares, the stadiums, and the streets, allowing the devil to spread sin and suffering. Let us not give up any of the rights or responsibilities that we have as Christians.

God has given us the power to conquer the land. And yet, what we have seen and heard is nothing compared to what He wants to give us. The truths of God must be proclaimed in every direction across the globe so that Satan is forced to quit his lying—and we alone are empowered to carry His message of hope. May God's words burn in our hearts until they can no longer be kept within the walls of our buildings, and may His message overcome all barriers. The North, the South, the East, and the West must hear the message of the Gospel.

We need to preach with courage and boldness, just like the early Christians, who often ended up in jail. God wants us to confront and fight against sin, rather than the sinner. And who is the one behind the sin? The one who came to steal, kill, and destroy. (John 10:10)

God has not changed and Jesus Christ is the same yesterday and today and forever. (Hebrews 13:8) Lord, enable us to preach your Word with great boldness just as Your first believers did. "Now, Lord, consider their threats and enable your servants to speak your word with great boldness. Stretch out your hand to heal and perform signs and wonders through the name of your holy servant Jesus." (Acts 4: 19-20)

CHAPTER 7

A Call to Spiritual Maturity

When I was young, and before I knew the Lord, my work was the most important thing in my life. I wanted my family to have a good standard of living and never want for anything. And so by hard work and continuous effort I built up a business in the city where I lived.

It began as a hardware store, but as the business grew and prospered, I specialized in the supply of tools and machinery to industrial enterprises. Looking back over the years, I can see how the Lord has prospered my business to enable me to finance evangelistic campaigns all across Argentina.

Consequently, whenever I was not away on a campaign, I would be working in the business helping to move things forward. I would often bring some of my children to work with me because there were always lots of exciting things going on. While I would be in the office, signing papers or having meetings, they would be running around the sprawling property getting into mischief. Their fun usually ended up making a mess in the area where they were playing.

They especially enjoyed the section that was filled with boxes of all kinds of screws, nuts and bolts, and washers, etc., each one labelled by their size and type. Their favorite game was for one of them to hop on one of the trolleys that was used for transporting loads around the store, while the other would push the trolley at high speed through the narrow aisles. This usually ended up with them crashing into a wall of meticulously organized boxes, which would come crashing down in a shower of screws, washers, and nuts and bolts, leaving them scattered across the floor.

While this was great fun for my kids, the store assistant responsible for keeping that particular area tidy took a different view. The first I would hear about it, however, would be when one or more of my kids would trudge woefully into my office complaining that so-and-so had twisted their ear. The store employees would frequently have to chase my kids out of their various areas, or sometimes even drag them away!

As my kids grew older though, they started to assume responsibility for different areas of the family business. When they were young they would have their hair pulled or their ears twisted, but once they grew up, they would start to give instructions to the employees and take charge of different departments.

From the beginning, my children were the heirs of the business, but they did not have the maturity or the ability to exercise their authority as the owners. However, once they reached adulthood, they put childish things behind them and started to behave like the rightful owners and managers of the business that they were.

What I have just related is a picture of what happens in our Christian lives. When we first accept Jesus as Lord, we are born again, and like infant babies, we depend on others to care for us. Although all the blessings of God's Kingdom are available to us, we rely on others to help us receive them because our own understanding is limited. Although we are legitimate heirs of the Kingdom, in reality we don't act like it.

The Bible explains the situation like this in Galatians 3:29-4:1, **"**If you belong to Christ, then you are Abraham's seed, and heirs according to the promise. What I am saying is that as long as an heir is under age, he is no different from a slave, although he owns the whole estate."

There are areas of our Christian lives where we have not yet reached a sufficient level of maturity to exercise the authority that Jesus has given us. This is not what God desires. It might have been many years since we were born again, but we may still be acting like spiritual children. Although we are heirs and masters of all, we are living like slaves and not experiencing the life of freedom and spiritual influence that Christ offers.

One of the signs of spiritual immaturity in the life of a believer is that the person can't achieve the freedom required to live a life of victory. They live as slaves, and the circumstances that dominate their lives push them one way and then the other, preventing them from moving forward. This spiritual immaturity can also be found in the Church, which is the body of Christ. Although we should be taking charge of the spiritual world, we often find ourselves getting distracted by childish things.

As I travel around the world preaching the wonderful message of salvation, I often come across churches distracted by unimportant matters while pain and suffering are intensifying all around them. Selfishness, pride, jealousy, envy, gossip, one person pitting themselves against another, accusations, unresolved conflicts, children of God commanded to love, yet who refuse to talk to one another, to meet together, to work together, or to forgive one another... It is just awful! Some think that their group is more numerous or better than others, while others feel that their group has fewer, and are looked down on. These different traditions, ways of thinking, and ways of working divide and alienate us.

Symptoms of spiritual immaturity, these godless woes present us with a challenge that we need to surmount. The time has come to lay aside the unimportant matters such childish arguments, and start to work together in love as Jesus taught us.

The previous passage from Galatians shows us a wonderful spiritual truth. Although a child might be the heir and owner of the whole estate, it doesn't have the ability to exercise the authority that has been given to it. So the father waits until the right time, until he sees that the child has developed a sufficient level of maturity and experience. We can't remain at the level of spiritual children all our lives. We need to grow up and mature in the Lord, in order to exercise the authority that God has given us in Jesus.

In Him we have recovered the authority to overcome the devil and to bring about change. The Church of Jesus Christ has the authority to be a fountain of blessing and reverse the destructive work of the enemy. This authority has been given to us; all that remains for us to do is grow up in God, believe that He has given it to us, and start to exercise it. By doing this, we will see changes in our lives that can include entire cities, and even nations. The Scripture reinforces this reality of who we are when it declares, "So you are no longer a slave, but God's child; and since you are his child, God has made you also an heir." (Galatians 4:7)

All that I am sharing here is the product of over thirty-years of ministry. It is not based on extensive research or reading around the subject. It is based solely on the reality of what I have experienced on the frontlines of the battle for the souls of the lost. God has taught us and helped us to live out each of the points expressed here. All these experiences help me to keep living according to what the Bible teaches. I know that these principles work and that they produce supernatural results by God's grace.

We believe that every biblical principle God has given us in His Word is there to be believed and applied, rather than merely understood. When we, as children of God, live according to what He has taught us, then these scriptural promises become living realities in our lives.

The hour has come for the Church to reach maturity, to leave behind childish things and work together so that the glory of God is reflected by us, among us, and through us. We can no longer allow Satan to hurt and hinder us. The day has dawned that we need to rise up as men and women of God and put Him in his place, the place that Jesus gave him. He has been conquered and the Church has authority over him. For us, Jesus has won a destiny of victory, but for our enemy, a destiny of defeat. It is time to take our rightful place in God. There is a world out there that is languishing, and has needs that grow more serious with every passing day. It is a world that is waiting for the sons of God to be revealed.

Will you be faithful with what God has given you and for which Jesus gave up His life?

Kill the Evangelist

By Pastor Hugo Alberto Basile

In October 2006, we went to the Argentine city of Santa Fe to do an evangelism campaign, which was scheduled to continue for many days. The Holy Spirit worked powerfully performing signs, wonders, and miracles; healing the sick and setting free those oppressed by the devil. Hundreds of people were set free from spiritual bondage, trauma, emotional wounds, and the suffering caused by sin, and transformed into a new life of light and fullness of the Holy Spirit.

I remember the second last day of the campaign especially well. The weather was perfect that evening and thousands of people came to hear the Gospel at Federal Park, which provided the perfect setting. The atmosphere was one of joy and celebration as the evangelist gave a powerful message of new life and hope. Suddenly the peace and jubilation were shattered by the loud bellowing of an enormous man who was rushing to the front, pushing and growling at everyone in his way. He appeared to have a supernatural strength due to the legion of demons that controlled his mind and will—and which both terrified and enthralled all those standing nearby.

The fearsome behemoth came right up to the platform, and using his hands, raised the one-and-a-half ton structure on which the evangelist was standing, about four-inches off the ground. Everyone who saw what was happening pushed back as they tried to get away from the terrifying spectacle.

The evangelist, perched atop the tilting platform responded by taking authority in the name of Jesus. "Satan, devil, I bind you in the name Jesus Christ of Nazareth!" Immediately the legions of demons that controlled him were unable to move. Throughout the remainder of the message and the altar call, this enormous figure was left standing there immobilized.

When the time came for the prayers of deliverance, the evangelist rebuked all unclean spirits present, and the powerful man was instantly knocked to the ground, turning over several times in the process. Several volunteers were soon on the scene to assist him to the deliverance tent where he received ministry.

This man was possessed by Satan and needed the freedom that only Jesus can give. In the tent, several volunteers ministered to him with love and compassion in the authority of Jesus. After he understood his need for salvation and freedom, he repented of his sins, and confessed and renounced each one breaking the agreements that he had made with the devil.

The list was long: family curses which had held his life in bondage were broken; he was set free from agreements with practitioners of the occult; he renounced all hatred, roots of bitterness, all sexual sins, and all the things that bound him to Satan. After several hours of ministry, he was completely free.

Later the same evening, he came to see the evangelist, and with tears in his eyes, he asked forgiveness for what had happened that night. He was ashamed of what the devil had done with his life and how Satan had used him to do his work. He explained that earlier the same day, that his mother, who was a priestess of Satan because of a covenant she had made with the devil, was given the clear command to "kill the evangelist." However, what Satan had intended for evil, Jesus had transformed for good, glorifying God by salvation and freedom.

–Hugo Alberto Basile
Pastor and member of the ministry of
Carlos Annacondia, Message of Salvation.

"Mar del Plata Jesus Loves You"

By Pastor Omar Olier

In 1978, God spoke to me personally, telling me that that He was going to give us the city of Mar del Plata. Although I didn't understand very much about what He meant, in faith, I began to pray and fast once a week for the burden that the Lord had put on my heart. As time passed, from my position on the staff of a local church, I failed to see any sign of what the Lord had told me was going to happen.

Year after year, God continued to confirm the word through dreams and visions given to other local Christians, in which He said He was going to do something big in the city of Mar del Plata. In response to this, we conducted evangelistic meetings, we kept fasting and praying, and in faith we prepared ourselves for the time when God would fulfil what He had promised.

One day, news reached us from the city of La Plata, near Buenos Aires, of a man that God had raised up, and whom He was using in an incredible way. We wanted to see if what they said was really happening. Perhaps this could be the man whom God would use to bring revival to our city. Thus, with a tremendous expectation we travelled to the city of La Plata.

All that we saw at the campaign had a huge impact on us, particularly the way that the evangelism and ministry were conducted. We immediately began to make plans for the ministry of Carlos Annacondia to come to our city, but it was not easy. What we had to overcome was a requirement of the ministry that the campaign needed to be organized by a group of united local churches. Many of the pastors in Mar del Plata knew nothing about the ministry, and many of those that did, didn't agree with it. Ours was a challenging task that required prayer and perseverance. But finally, on October 19th, 1984, the campaign titled "Mar del Plata, Jesus loves you" with the evangelist Carlos Annacondia, began.

It was a great privilege to get to know Carlos Annacondia personally during the preparations for the event, something that was foundational for me as my own ministry began to gather momentum. Through time spent with him and his family over meals, I came to realize that God is sovereign and does as He wants. Titles and qualifications are not important to Him. Here was a man who had an incredible burden for lost souls, a man with an extremely tender heart that was intimately in touch with God—I had never seen anything like it.

I was struck by his commitment, the authority he had in deliverance, and the incredible gift of faith he exercised in healing, which became apparent during the campaign. The most striking thing of all was that his undeniable authority was accompanied by a deep humility and a willingness to share with others all that he had received by God's grace. This really blessed me.

Carlos' friendship and ministry transformed my life. He passed on his ministry, and continues to do so to those who are prepared to receive it and use it in the service of the Lord. Wherever he went, he imparted the same anointing to others. This set him apart from any other evangelist that I had met up until that time. Evangelists used to come to our city, preach at a meeting, and after they left, any sign of revival would disappear. But Carlos was different.

Many pastors and Christian leaders discuss the work of God in their cities in terms of "Before Annacondia's visit" and "After Annacondia's visit." Mar del Plata is no exception! At the start of my ministry back in 1978, I saw the city as a wheat field ready for harvest. But after 1984, I came to see things differently; the heads of the wheat stalks were no longer pointing upwards, but were pointing downwards, signifying their ripeness. All that remained to be done was to harvest the crop and prepare the barns for storing the grain. Those who go out onto the streets to harvest in obedience to God's commands will not return empty handed. By God's grace, as we did this, God responded, and was faithful.

The ministry of Carlos Annacondia, more than any other evangelist that I have ever known or studied, is an instrument of God to increase the growth rate of churches involved in their campaigns. Dr. Peter Wagner states, "After more than twenty-years of study of city-wide evangelism campaigns, I can say that no other ministry has produced such a steady stream of testimonies." I can attest that this happened in the city of Mar del Plata.

I had never seen any other campaign evangelist confront demonic powers so forcefully in public. The campaign meetings were filled with a remarkable power and anointing. The healings and miracles that occurred were like what we see in the Book of Acts. These manifestations of God's presence had a profound effect on our city. Here are some of the testimonies:

- Rosa Colasanto, who lives in the city's center, was diagnosed with breast cancer a few months before the start of the campaign. At one of the meetings, she fell down under the power of the Holy Spirit and the cancerous tumor disappeared miraculously. Thirty-years later she is serving the Lord and testifying to what the He has done.

- Olga Cosmano, who lives in the Las Americas neighborhood, received a miracle in her teeth. During one of the meetings, the whole of the inside of the upper arch was covered in a platinum-like substance.

- Norma Ramirez, from the Florencio Sánchez district, came to a meeting suffering from a tumor located between her bladder and urethra. This disappeared completely during the prayers for healing.

- Juliano Vilches, from the Libertad neighborhood, was healed of epilepsy.

- Fausto Reinoso, aged nine and completely deaf, recovered his hearing instantly.

- Angelica Momoli, was healed of tuberculosis and asthma.

These are just a few of the countless testimonies of the power and love of God. Even pedestrians walking near the campaign site fell down under the power of the Holy Spirit.

The ministry of Carlos Annacondia added a new emphasis on spiritual warfare and deliverance to our ongoing work of evangelism that we had not known up until that time. We learned to proclaim the Gospel, not only to people, but also to the spiritual jailers that hold them captive, ordering them to let their prisoners go in the name of Jesus.

At last I was able to see the fulfilment of God's promise to me. Not only were 83,054 souls entrusted to us, but we also received the city. In the more than thirty-years since the campaign, we have been able to reap the fruits of perseverance and effort. Today the results are clear for all to see.

At the time of the campaign, there were twenty churches in the city and today, there are more than two-hundred. The harvest continues. We have a weekly meeting of the pastoral committee comprised of some fourteen members, and a monthly meeting with all the churches.

Over the last ten-years we have been joined by pastors from neighboring cities. We can declare that, even today, the work of salvation, healing, and miracles goes on. But above all, we know the authority we have over the enemy by which God gives us power to bind and loose, and bring about the fall of the kingdom of darkness.

–Omar Olier,
Pastor, God is Love Christian Center,
Mar del Plata, Buenos Aires, Argentina

Testimonies

The Restoration of a Family

When his mother was fourteen-years old, she became pregnant through a relationship with an older man. Eventually the man left, and when he did, she wanted nothing to do with the child who was ruining her life. This was how Nestor's life began, so it's hardly surprising that he has no memories of love or happiness in his childhood.

Soon after his fifth birthday, his mother moved in with another man, who turned out to be violent towards Nestor and his mother. This man also had a son that was continually favored over Nestor who felt like he had been abandoned for the second time in his life.

Nestor suffered terribly from the continual mistreatment of his step-father. The slightest thing would cause him to fly into a rage and drag Nestor across the room by the hair, or beat him about the head. The daily insults he endured made him feel totally humiliated. During PE class at school, he had to make excuses for the bruises on his leg which were the result of beatings with an iron cable.

By the time he was thirteen-years old, he had had enough violence and mistreatment. So one day he confronted his stepfather and threatened to cut off his head with a knife during the night if he laid another hand on him. From that time on the beatings stopped, but his life did not get any better.

He started to hang out on the streets with guys who were in their twenties or thirties and get into trouble with them. Desperately searching for happiness and an escape from his miserable past, he started to visit brothels and get involved in all kinds of perversion.

After some time, he was able to get a decent job and a steady girlfriend, but instead of feeling happy, he felt more and more depressed. The only way that he could face each day was by downing two litres of beer before going to work.

Sometimes he would find himself asking, "Where are you God?" Everyone around him seemed to have a normal family, something that was a pipe dream for him. Since he thought that his life had no future, one day he made the tragic decision to end it. He climbed up onto a towering bridge in the city of Olavarria where he lived to do just that. He could hear an inner voice urging him to, "Throw yourself off! It's the only way you'll find peace." But something stopped him and he couldn't go through with it. He was often tempted to slash his wrists with one of the large knives he used at the bakery where he worked.

One day his girlfriend, Monica, announced that she was pregnant. Nestor was only nineteen, but he was determined not to repeat the mistakes of his parents, and so they got married. But even though they did everything they could to make married life a success, they soon realized that history was repeating itself. The first two-years of marriage were marred by arguments and violence until it seemed that the only solution was separation.

Monica was the last in a long line of brothers and sisters. She always sensed that her life was unplanned and unwanted, leading to deep feelings of rejection. The lack of love she had experienced in childhood left her unable to offer any kind of affection towards others, her family included. At eighteen-years old she was certainly not ready to be a wife and mother.

But one day, Monica's sister invited them both to a lunch at the evangelical church that she attended. At first, Nestor would have none of it because he had always felt abandoned by God. But when his sister-in-law persisted in inviting him, he agreed to go with Monica. "What touched me was the deep love I saw between the people who were present," he recalled. "It was the first time in my life that I had experienced anything like this."

Shortly afterwards, an evangelism campaign began in the neighbouring city of Azul. Their new friends at the church told Nestor and Monica that there would be miracles, healings, and all kinds of amazing things. The two of them decided to go, thinking it was just an outing with some friends from the church.

They arrived at the campaign site to find a huge crowd singing joyful choruses with their arms raised in worship. They listened to Carlos Annacondia preaching about the love of Jesus, and then came the moment for the altar call. Nestor and Monica looked at each other as they considered how to respond. They both knew that if they did not go forward together, they would end up going their separate ways. This was their last chance; there was no alternative but to accept Jesus into their hearts! So taking each other by the hand, they went to the altar to give their lives to the Lord. They had decided to give God a chance to restore them and give them a fresh start.

Until that point, Nestor had always blamed others for the problems in his life. But now, for the first time, he owned up to his mistakes. "I don't remember much of the message," he admitted. "What I do remember is the evangelist saying, 'All your sins are forgiven! God does not remember them anymore!' And I believed it. It was what I needed to hear."

When the evangelist began to pray for deliverance, the two of them fell to the ground, and lay there for several minutes. The next thing they remember is hearing Carlos give a call to service as he said, "God has great plans for your life." Nestor responded by dedicating his life to Jesus, so that the Lord could do with it what He thought best. "Lord, here I am. Please use me," the newly saved man prayed!

"I was in floods of tears," he recalled. He couldn't stop crying all the way home, with his wife by his side. The night that he accepted Jesus into his heart was the happiest night of his life. For the first time ever, he felt a peace and a joy in his heart. The change was immediate as the visit to the campaign produced a complete about face in Nestor. Step by step, God transformed his personal life and marriage for the better. He received a deep love for Jesus and a tremendous conviction of sin.

His wife was also strengthened in her faith as she watched the changes taking place in her husband's life. He had always been fascinated by martial arts, but from that moment on, he realized that God was not pleased with that, among many other things.

From that day on, despite the many challenges that they have faced together, Nestor and Monica have never given up serving the Lord. Over the last twenty-five years, they have continued to attend the same church where they first heard the message of the love of Jesus. They are now the pastors of that fellowship and have three beautiful daughters, all professionals, who share the faith of their parents.

"For many years I believed that my life would be short and sad," says Nestor "But now I realize that brother Annacondia was right when he said 'God has great plans for your life!'"

HEALED OF AIDS

For five long years, depression, abuse, and the prognosis of death were my constant companions. There was no hope for me or the child that I was carrying. We were living in the early years of the AIDS epidemic and understanding about the disease was painfully lacking.

I had watched a friend die of this terrible disease, which deprives a person of their senses one by one. I stared heartbroken at the confusion in the faces of her children as they tried to come to terms with why their mother had to die. For me there would be no more Christmases or New Year's Eve celebrations, and my son would never know the mother who loved him so much.

A friend once told me about the evangelism campaigns of the Message of Salvation ministry, where many were healed and set free. Ever since, I had never stopped asking "Are there going to be any campaigns? When is there going to be another campaign?" Finally, my friend had some good news for me, and she agreed to take me along to a campaign that was being held in a suburb of Buenos Aires called Moreno.

I hardly had the strength to walk, but with my friend's help, we made it to the site of the campaign. When the time came for the altar call, I felt something propel me forward with all of the others who gathered in front of the platform. During the prayers for healing, the evangelist placed his hands on my head, and I was instantly filled with an incredible peace. My mind became much clearer, and I knew something had happened.

A few days later, my wonderful son, Joel, was born. I'll never forget the incredible happiness I felt when the doctors told me that he did not have HIV; he was completely healthy. At least for him, there was a future of life and hope. Unfortunately, I was still forced to take higher and higher doses of medication to try and combat the effects of AIDS in my own body.

Sometime later, I was invited to another campaign, this time a bit further away. But I made the journey carrying my baby son in my arms because I knew that only a miracle could save me. Even before getting off the bus that took us to the site, I could hear the choruses of faith and hope that the crowd was enthusiastically singing. Some were clapping, others had their hands held high in worship, and many testified to what Jesus had done in their lives.

That night, the evangelist told the story of a blind man named Bartimaeus who loudly cried out for healing, "Jesus, Son of David, have mercy on me." (Mark 10:47) His cry was the same as mine, a cry that came from years spent in tears crying and groaning. When the time came for the altar call, I heard the invitation, "Come, Jesus is calling you!" I literally ran through the crowds in desperation, with my baby in my arms. I knelt and prayed with all my heart. Jesus heard my cry for healing from the disease that had put an end to my dreams. I knew that God had touched me.

I went back to see the doctors and they did extensive tests to see if I still had AIDS. But they could find no trace of the virus in my body. They can confirm that I have been completely healed. That was more than ten-years ago, and in that time I have not needed any treatment. Low immunity and all the problems that go with AIDS now belong to the past. What happened to me was not just something emotional. I am living the healing and restoring power of Jesus Christ and I have never felt more fulfilled than I do now.

My husband and my oldest son have also experienced the power of God. Friends and neighbors who witnessed my darkest days have also come to receive Jesus Christ as Lord because of His amazing grace to me through salvation and healing.

Some time ago I was baptized, and I attend a church in the Ciudadela neighborhood of Buenos Aires. I work on a daily radio program, and give testimony to what Jesus has done in my life. Now it's the turn of others to ask, "Sandra, are there going to be any campaigns? When is there going to be another campaign?"

Set Free from Childhood Trauma

"One day you will serve the Lord!" These were the words that set off the sequence of events that brought Jesus into Margarita's life. A street sweeper who used to clean the road in front of her house stopped her one day to give her this message from Jesus, "You are going to serve the Lord!" he said insistently. In her desperate state, this was something she found very hard to believe, and so she answered him with a mocking laugh. But the man was not deterred, and he repeated several times that the Lord had a plan for Margarita and that one day she would be a servant of God.

No one had ever told her that something good could come of her life which was why she responded as she did—she just couldn't believe it was true. For as long as she could remember, her life had been full of suffering and pain. She lived her childhood in the kind of home that no one would wish to grow up in.

Together with her mother and sister, she was a victim of the destruction that drugs and alcohol wreak on a family. They could only relax when their father was out of the house, but his return always loomed with a dark foreboding and the promise of suffering. Margarita's mother, traumatized by the savagery that their drunk and drugged father made them endure, used to try and hide her daughters. But with threats and blows, he would soon find their hiding place and drag the little girls out to be insulted and abused.

For a girl her age, Margarita had already gone through more than her fair share of suffering. She would hear an unrelenting voice within that used to confuse and frighten her with the words, "Kill yourself! Kill yourself!" This haunting voice was so strong, and her suffering so great, that one day as she was lying in her room, she set fire to the mattress, hoping to be trapped by the flames. But much to her regret, the firefighters arrived in time and managed to extinguish the blaze. Her childhood was the worst nightmare that anyone could imagine.

Margarita was five-years old when her mother decided to escape the constant fear and anxiety so she took the two girls away from the village of their birth and moved to another city in Mexico. It was a tremendous relief to be away from their violent father, but her solace was short lived, and the pain and suffering were soon to continue.

Because Margarita's mother had to work all day long to support her daughters, the girls were locked alone in a small room so that no one could harm them. Later their mother arranged for an aunt to stay with them and take care of the girls. What she didn't know was that the girls' pain and suffering continued. The poor children had to stay in the room while their aunt had sexual relations with the various men that used to visit.

Realizing that she could not look after them, their mother took the girls back to their home village, and left them with their father. The only person who had appeared to love them was gone, and they again suffered a relentless barrage of insults, abuse, and suffering day after day. Terror once more ruled Margarita's life, as she became a victim of her father's advances. He never viewed her as his daughter, but as a woman whose purpose was to satisfy his desires.

When Margaret was fifteen, she was surprised when her mother returned seeking them. She was no longer alone, but had started another family with a husband and newborn child. Trying to live all together as a family again was difficult for Margaret and her sister. They didn't feel as if they fit into this new home, and their mother only had time for the baby.

Once she reached the age of seventeen, Margaret thought that things would get better if she could start her own family. That was how she came to marry a young man, not out of love, but to try and escape an unhappy home with a history of anxiety and pain. But the chains that had bound her since childhood continued to hold her captive. Looking for a means of escape, they decided to move to the United States but nothing was different. Once she realized that having her own husband and family could not change the reality of her situation, she went out into the street with the same idea that had haunted her since childhood—taking her life.

It was with this thought in mind that she bumped into a neighbor who suggested something to her that seemed the answer to her problems. That was why she agreed to accompany him to what she thought at first was a church service. But as the meeting went on, she began to feel uneasy. Thankfully she was able to leave what turned out to be an occultic ritual before its members were able to harm her.

Over the next few months she tried all kinds of things that promised solutions to her problems, including parapsychologists and mediums. She made several other unsuccessful attempts to end her life until, finally exhausted, she gave up all hope of ever finding an escape from her past.

It was then that she recalled the words that the sweeper had spoken to her, "You are going to serve the Lord!" With tears of despair streaming down her face, Margarita got down on her knees in her room and began to pray, "Lord Jesus, if it is true that you exist, please come into my life! Change me. I need your love because so far no one else has been able to provide it! I don't want go on like this."

At that moment, she felt the presence of God very intensely and something inside her changed forever. She felt like a new person. When she saw her husband, she fell in love with him; he seemed different. She thought, "What beautiful children God has given me! What a beautiful family I have!"

From that day on, the Lord began to restore her life. She and her family began to attend a church; God's love filled her home and many things changed. However, Margarita just couldn't break free from the past. The things that she had lived through were so strong that they never ceased to torment her. Their memories produced so much distress that it was continuously overwhelming.

After two-years of knowing the Lord and allowing Him into her life, Margarita was invited to attend a church where two brothers from Argentina were going to pray for deliverance. At first, she thought that it wouldn't be good to go to the meeting, but then the Lord spoke to her and said "I need you to be there. I have something for you."

So, in obedience to the voice of God, she went along to the meeting. When the brothers began to teach about deliverance, Margarita's initial reaction was to reject the idea. "I don't need this. God has already forgiven me," she thought. But, despite her doubts, she asked for prayer to be freed from the past and agreed to receive ministry. After renouncing all of her sins, including the hatred and resentment she felt towards those who had harmed her, Margarita felt complete freedom!

Looking back on the experience several years later, Margarita observed, "Now I understand what it takes to be free. In the name of Jesus, I had to renounce all my sins of the past, the bitterness and hatred, and all impurity. Now I understand why the Bible says, 'My people are destroyed from lack of knowledge.' (Hosea 4:6) I am so grateful that the Lord led me and my husband to the place of deliverance. Now I am free for the glory of God. Jesus restored my life, and my family, and now we are serving Him together! Glory to God! The road sweeper's word to me has been fulfilled!"

VISION:
"Evangelize Argentina, America, and the world"

MISSION:
"Serve the local churches through the evangelistic crusades."

MANDATE:
"Leave the fruit of the crusades, the effort and united work within the churches so that they grow in the faith and power of God."

CarlosAnnacondia.com